Ohno

The Toyota Mindset

Ohno would be very angry to know how his former students messed up the company 1998-2009

- *The Ten Commandments of Taiichi Ohno* -

The Toyota Mindset

- The Ten Commandments of Taiichi Ohno -

Yoshihito Wakamatsu

Address all comments and inquiries to:

Enna Products Corporation
1602 Carolina St.
Unit B3
Bellingham, WA 98229
Telephone: (360) 306-5369
Fax: (905) 481-0756
E-mail: info@enna.com

Printed in the United States of America

Library of Congress Control Number: 2009938286

Library of Congress Cataloging-in-Publication Data
Wakamatsu, Yoshihito
The Toyota Mindset
 Includes index.
 ISBN 978-1-926537-11-5
 1. Operations Management 2. Management Productivity 3. Management Quality 4. Management Efficiency

Written by Yoshihito Wakamatsu

English Translator: Junpei Nakamuro
Illustrator: Khemanand Shiwram
Editor: Collin McLoughlin
Associate Editor: Shawna Gilleland

Contents

Publisher's Note

Taiichi Ohno is often described as a person who was loud, in your face, and absolutely brilliant. Commonly known as the founder of the Toyota Production System, Ohno was a man who believed unwaveringly in his ability to get people to use their intellect to solve the problems of the shop floor.

The stories and examples recounted in this book provide valuable insight into his belief, as well as giving a glimpse into the transitional period of Toyota's history that led to them becoming a world leader in manufacturing. There are not many other books out there that can give a reader such an in-depth look at the man who revolutionized the way manufacturing is done.

Another reason this book is such an invaluable addition to any library of Lean or Toyota Production System books, is the fact that it shows you the reasons *behind* the way things are done. You are provided with stories of how

Ohno devised the now common standards of practice. Not only do we get to see how his mind operated and how he dealt with people on a regular basis, but also the reasoning behind his decisions. The revolutionary ideas that he generated remain unsurpassed in their vision of streamlined efficiency. These ideas, these gems of wisdom, are what make this book magnificent.

I decided to have this book translated based on a number of factors, not the least of which was the fact that it gets right to the heart of how the Toyota Production System came into being. There is no in-depth discussion of principles, merely descriptions of how these principles came to be. What events took place to bring these fundamental tools into being? Why did the standard of practice change? Such are the questions this book answers.

Many people who have read about Taiichi Ohno and the Toyota Production System ask themselves, "What would Ohno do in a situation like this?" After reading this book you will be better able to answer that question and many more.

The stories include both the people who were invaluable to the birth of the system and the challenges that they needed to overcome to make it possible. It is my hope that by engaging in a deeper understanding, and using the knowledge that is given in this book, you will be better equipped to deal with situations and problems that may arise within your own company.

It is my hope that you will cherish this invaluable guide to the inner workings of a brilliant mind and enjoy reading this book as much as I did.

Collin McLoughlin
Publisher

Foreword

In Culman Co., LTD, many of my colleagues, as well as myself, worked under Taiichi Ohno in the past. When we talk about Taiichi Ohno everyone remembers him as an intimidating person. When he would inspect our shop floor while we were conducting continuous improvement, we often found ourselves hiding from him behind machinery. We would avoid eye contact with him so that he would not initiate conversation with any of us. Every once in a while, we ran out of luck and were pinpointed by him. In that case, as I will describe in detail in this book, Ohno would throw work-in-progress items at us with great intensity.

He would sometimes order us to do things that were puzzling to us. He would tell us, "Go stand in a circle and observe the shop floor for a while," or "Follow me around while holding this box in your arms." Some workers even saw him cut a tie in half, worn by a staff member that happened to be wandering around the shop floor.

We were young and innocent shop floor workers back then. We hardly understood Ohno's strange behaviors and just concentrated on meeting his expectations by trying our hardest to solve problems with our own ideas.

The next thing that my colleagues often mention is that the way they looked at Ohno changed dramatically once they had left Toyota. It was when we became consultants for adapting the Toyota System in many companies and factories outside of Toyota that we discovered the true implications and magnitude of what Ohno was trying to teach us over the years. To this day Toyota principles continue to be the common practice for many manufacturing industries.

The transformation within a production system is realized progressively by establishing mutual understanding among those who possess different philosophies. By accomplishing these processes on our own we become capable of translating his words in the right way and acknowledging that he too had faced the same challenges in the past. We all appreciate his effort from the bottom of our hearts and contribute our success to his commitment to teaching us his principles on the shop floor.

When Fujio Cho was the president of Toyota, he gave a recommendation to my first book, titled "Toyota's Production System and Empowerment of the Workers." At the same time he paid his greatest tribute to Ohno by saying, "Ohno was an extraordinary leader, as well as an educator, who never lost faith in his beliefs or his workers." I could not agree more.

The Toyota Production System, as well as its application to larger-scale production improvement, has attracted a great deal of attention among many industries in recent years. Books, including my own, that help us learn about the transformation always mention the name "Taiichi Ohno." In addition, when faced with difficult challenges and situations in which the right judgment is not easily reached, many people around me often seek answers by reading Ohno's books, such as *The Toyota Production System*, and try putting themselves in his shoes to derive effective solutions — as he had in the past.

This is the magnitude of influence that Ohno had over the Toyota System. Thus, it is obvious that people desire to study in more detail his personality and his way of thinking, as well as how work should be performed under his guidance. That is the very reason why I decided to write the 10 Commandments, which are strictly based on Taiichi Ohno's philosophy.

It is true that Ohno did not throw out the 10 Commandments in the same way as I have described in this book. The 10 Commandments are described, in my own words, into 10 main ideas that are based accurately on Toyota's way of thinking and the work ethic that I have learned over the years, both from Ohno and as a Toyota worker and consultant.

In some cases, Ohno would deny some of the ideas found in the 10 Commandments. However, I strongly doubt that the 10 Commandments are very far off from his original way of thinking. I have been straightforward to convey my real experiences and knowledge, which helped me to learn the difficulties of work and the degree of commitment required for achieving goals.

The most important element is to have faith in human intelligence and potential. Humans can be empowered by taking full advantage of their innate intelligence. This is the unbreakable foundation upon which Ohno's beliefs were built. *What training is missing on the shop floors these days?* Many leaders have failed to both challenge their workers with hard-to-achieve goals and believe strongly in their intelligence and ability to grow.

Ohno would show his commitment by spending 3 straight days discovering the true cause of defects. My colleagues, who were found responsible for a defect, had received some serious scoldings from him. However, it was an inevitable reaction toward them as Ohno strongly believed that defects should never reach the hands of customers whatsoever.

He also went as far as believing that producing defects equaled wasting the lives of responsible workers. These beliefs helped workers endure hardships and later discover the extraordinary essence behind Ohno's philosophy.

I want readers to utilize the 10 Commandments as a starting point. There is nothing more rewarding than having Ohno's principles, described in this book, be realized by readers as a way of creating stronger organizations and higher self-esteem.

- Yoshihito Wakamatsu, President of Culman Co., LTD.

The 10 Commandments

I. WASTES HIDE SO START BY DISCLOSING ALL OF YOUR MISTAKES

II. DISCOVER THE TRUTH BEYOND YOUR UNDERSTANDING

III. INCREASING PRODUCTION WHILE LIMITING THE NUMBER OF WORKERS IS THE ONLY WAY TO GAIN TRUE SUCCESS

IV. ACT ON PROBLEMS RIGHT AWAY, DON'T PROCRASTINATE

V. DON'T FEEL SATISFIED BY SAYING, "I FINISHED THE JOB" GO BEYOND THAT AND SAY, "I CAN DO MORE"

VI. ADD "APPROPRIATE TIMING" TO "APPROPRIATE METHOD" IN PROBLEM-SOLVING

VII. BELIEVE IN "I CAN" AND QUESTION "I CAN'T"

VIII. THE KEY TO ACHIEVING PROGRESS IS TO NEVER GIVE UP

IX. DON'T DO WORK AT AN AVERAGE PACE; THE SHORTEST WAY IS ALWAYS THE EASIEST

X. CHANGE YOURSELF FIRST IF YOU WANT TO CHANGE SOMEONE ELSE

Commandment 1

"You are a cost. Eliminate wastes first, for that is the
only way for you to develop your potential."

WASTES HIDE SO START BY DISCLOSING ALL OF YOUR MISTAKES

DO NOT HIDE DEFECTS

The creator of the Toyota Production System (also
know as the Toyota System), Taiichi Ohno appeared
intimidating to every one, including myself. In fact, he was
a truly compassionate man whose words were always correct. He was always full of a radiance that is unique to
those whose level of dedication toward creating innovative methods is extremely high.

One of the characteristics of the Toyota System is elimination of wastes in an absolute manner, and there are
many categories of wastes to be removed. Most impor-
tantly, eliminating defects is the key strategy for improving the production cost, quality, and delivery of finished

products.

In the 1950's, when the Toyota System was first practiced in production, Ohno was on everybody's back and persistently ordered workers to present defects in front of everybody's eyes. When defects occurred, the shop floor workers had a habit of storing them away in places where nobody could easily find them. This was because defects often led supervisors to question the skills of the responsible worker, which was the main reason why Ohno's orders remained unrealized on the shop floor.

One day, Ohno stepped into the shop floor. Workers were always intimated by him and continued to perform their jobs without making eye contact.

> Ohno suddenly jumped into the production line and asked with anger, "What in the world are these?"

The line leader approached Ohno to find that he was pointing his finger at the pile of work-in-progress items in the corner. Ohno began to scold the shop floor.

> "These are all defects. Why are these all hidden away? I told you so many times to place the defects where everyone can see and stop production entirely. "

The line leader was apologetic, but Ohno never liked hearing excuses. We never figured out how he got the strength to lift up all the defects and start throwing them into the hallway, until they were all gone from his arms. One of the defects even hit the head of the line leader but Ohno did not care about that at all.

> He stressed again, screaming, "Never hide defects! Bring them out into the hallway so that everyone can see."

After that, he left the shop floor. The line leader was left standing in front of his workers, which must have been quite embarrassing. If this still happens these days then it must have been a serious issue in the work place back then, though the shop floors at the time were much more roughly-mannered. I still remember the intensity of Ohno in this kind of situation quite vividly.

IT IS WASTEFUL TO CORRECT DEFECTS

Why was Ohno so fixated on the idea of disclosing defects so that everyone could see them? When a mistake occurs, or defect in this case, humans have a tendency to hide it away and try to resolve it later. They do not go out of their ways to stop the entire production line or process so that it can be dealt with immediately upon discovery. That is the main reason why the true cause of defects is never discovered. In this manner, the same defect continues to emerge, as no effective solutions can be formulated to eliminate the cause. This is a huge waste.

In addition, it is essentially a waste to correct defects later on. If defects are found on a given day and solutions cannot be formulated until the next day, then the time between the discovery of the defects and a solution is simply wasted. In this case, a whole day. This is the very reason why Ohno demanded to disclose all defects, so that workers had an opportunity to question themselves about why such defects occurred in the first place and discovered the true cause. The true cause lies beyond what can be seen on the surface and is the fundamental element that leads to mistakes.

He also stressed the importance of conducting continuous improvement repeatedly, with the involvement of every worker, so that the same mistakes could never occur again. For example, say that a defect was made by assembling the wrong components in a certain assembly process. In such a case, the defect should not be hidden away but presented to everyone on the shop floor so that everyone can ask why the mistake was made and improve the process by continuous improvement, in a rather casual manner. Ohno strongly believed that a company could grow tremendously if such an effort was systemized and carried out at all times on the shop floor.

Many unexpected things can still happen to the actual place of work (gemba) no matter how much continuous improvement effort is made. For the shop floor environment, as far as human workers are concerned, certain conflicts continue to occur as result of the gap between the levels of expertise among workers. Even an expert worker can still make mistakes if he is feeling sick or simply in a bad mood. As far as machinery is concerned, no matter how much attention is given to its safety, machinery breakdown is still beyond our control. You may also find defects among the items that were delivered from your suppliers.

These are the reasons why the shop floor is often considered excellent as long as "the first run rate" scores around 97–98%. The first run rate determines the ratio of defect-free products against the defects, after a quality inspection. In this case, the waste associated with correcting defects is limited to only two to three percent of production.

In practice, even the best manufacturer in the world finds it extremely difficult to yield a first run rate of 100%. Some people joke around saying that the only way to achieve a zero-defect goal in production is to not run production lines at all.

In fact, many factories permit a certain percentage of defects to be produced and believe it to be unrealistic to achieve zero-defects, while at the same time promising 100% defect free products to consumers. What sets Ohno separate from these factories is that he denied these assumptions and strongly believed that it was realistic to do so. Consequently, he made sure that these 2 principles were in place to achieve a zero-defect goal:

(1) Visualization

When defects are found, the entire production line is stopped. Defects are then brought to the foreground so that every worker can learn from them.

(2) Repeat "Why?" 5 times

The true cause of defects must be pursued thoroughly and elimination of such a cause is carried out by continuous improvement.

Visualization has become one of the standard principles in the Toyota System. However, it was extremely challenging to implement Visualization when the Toyota System first came into practice. This was because the successful implementation of Visualization had to remove any fear from the workers; the fear that bringing defects to the foreground placed blame directly onto the workers responsible for them. For this reason, workers often tended to deal with their mistakes on their own. However, neither mistakes nor defects could have been eliminated in this manner.

Ohno successfully inculcated the Visualization principle in the shop floor workers to make sure that defects and mistakes became a collective wealth among them all, so that workers became capable of formulating solutions to remove wastes more effectively. At the same time, he was also committed to teaching workers to maintain a high level of awareness toward cost-management. I will explain this in detail in the next section.

REASONING BEHIND THE TOYOTA SYSTEM

In the Toyota System, processes build the quality into a product. Product quality is never enhanced by tightening standards used for an inspection. Inspections serve only one purpose; rejecting defects so that they do not reach the end-users. Every time a defect occurs you must repeatedly ask yourself "Why?" and eliminate the true cause. By doing that persistently your ability to produce only good products will be enhanced. That is what makes it true to say that processes build the quality into a product.

COLLECTING SMALL PARTS LETS YOU IDENTIFY BIGGER WASTES

WHAT WOULD YOU DO IF IT WAS MONEY?

"Hey you, Mr. A. Carry this box and follow me around," Ohno ordered Mr. A, while he was conducting continuous improvement activities on the shop floor in Toyota. Ohno began wandering about the floor before he even finished the sentence. Mr. A picked up a wooden part box he found nearby and started following Ohno.

In a situation like most people would ask to find out where they were being led to, however Mr. A wanted to avoid confrontation with Ohno as he knew how intimidating Ohno could be. Ohno continued to roam around the shop floor while studying every aspect of the factory. Workers on the shop floor continued their work without making eye contact with Ohno, as usual.

It was a strange scene for everyone to observe as Mr. A following Ohno ever so quietly. It was also a funny scene, in a way, but nobody dared to either laugh at him or ask Mr. A what was going on. Mr. A continued to follow Ohno without uttering a word. They spent a good amount of time circling the entire factory.

> Ohno finally turned to him, upon returning to the starting point, and asked, "Mr. A, didn't you realize that there were many components lying on the floor?"
>
> "Yes. I did notice some components lying on the floor," Mr. A replied.
>
> "If you did, why did you not pick them up?" Ohno asked again.
>
> "You just told me to follow you around. You never told me to pick up those components," Mr. A replied.

"Shame on you! Go around the factory again and pick them up!" Ohno instructed him with anger.

Mr. A hurried back down their trail thru the factory and picked up the components, placing them into the wooden box. He told himself that he should have been told to pick them up in the first place but he could never rebel against Ohno. His colleagues saw Mr. A picking up the components and asked what was going on. He replied by saying "I am just doing what I was told to do by Ohno." All they could do to help Mr. A was show him their sympathy. "Good luck, Mr. A…"

Mr. A went back to where Ohno was standing and showed him the wooden box. Ohno picked up one of the components from the box and asked Mr. A,

"Do you have any idea how much these components are costing us?"

Unfortunately, Mr. A was not knowledgeable about the price of each component at the time.

"I have no idea," he replied.

"I see. How about I tell you the cost for these items you just picked up? I want you to calculate the total cost based on that," Ohno told Mr. A.

Mr. A took out his abacus and started punching in numbers (electronic calculators did not exist at the time.) What was so impressive was that Ohno had remembered the exact prices, including cents, for every item in the large box of components. However, what was more striking was the result of the calculation. It was quite shocking to see how small bolts and screws could cost the factory such a large amount of money. Usually, these items were ignored as they only represented a fraction of the total cost on their own.

"Were you surprised to learn how much money we are wasting?" Ohno asked Mr. A.

"Yes indeed. It opened my eyes," Mr. A replied.

"I understand. Everyone ignores these small items because they are insignificant, but what would you do if they were money? I am sure you would pick them up before anyone else. Imagine how much money you could gather up at the end," Ohno told Mr. A.

Ohno did not say anything more about it to Mr. A. This experience became the most important lesson that Mr. A learned in his career.

There are many other shop floor episodes like this one. I, myself, was trained to be cost-conscious in this manner by Ohno.

VISUALIZATION OF COST HELPS YOU MANAGE UNNECESSARY COST

The Toyota System never plays a guessing game in determining the cost of producing certain items. The cost per product can be calculated in advance by taking into consideration the price of each component and other expenses, such as labor, storage spaces, and so on. Therefore, any reduction in cost can be easily witnessed as a result of continuous improvements in the production processes.

In order for Ohno to teach workers this lesson of becoming cost-conscious, sometimes drastic, or rather unique, methods were often used. One of the methods that he used was being able to recite from memory the exact prices for each and every item used in the factory, which no one else in the factory could do at the time.

The scenario of Mr. A, who followed Ohno around on the shop floor, is a great example. Workers became cost-conscious and developed a new approach to their work by picking up discarded items from the floor with their own hands.

It seems that humans can change their actions when it is

about money. If workers are fully aware of the production cost and their labor expenses, they will naturally learn to think a great deal about the shop floor and, at the same time, find better ways to conduct their work so that the overall cost will be diminished. On the other hand, workers often find their work unbearably redundant in the administrative sector, where the cost does not directly affect their operation.

Let me tell you a story about the delivery company that was a part of a large corporate affiliate group. In the past, workers did not care about costs and did everything as ordered by their parent company, who had helped them financially over the years. One day, the company was asked to become financially independent. At this point, workers calculated the cost for everything and analyzed methods for reducing the cost by changing how they drove their trucks (even how to step on the gas and clutch) and selecting more efficient delivery routes.

To reduce cost effectively it is essential that every worker foresees the cost. Visualization allows workers to identify problems diligently and approach their work with cost-sensitive minds, which leads to them becoming a great source of continuous improvement ideas. Since that bitter experience with Ohno, Mr. A began to approach his work and continuous improvement activities with a tremendous level of attention to every cost involved in the production process.

Cost-awareness among workers cannot be attained by simply ordering workers to save and eliminate costs that exist on the surface. It has to be done, and enforced, by clarifying every cost that is to be acknowledged by every worker.

REASONING BEHIND THE TOYOTA SYSTEM

The Toyota System advocates the principle of "Visualization of Cost." If you were bluntly told to reduce the cost mainly because the company was going through some hard times, you would neither take it seriously, nor change the way you perform work. However, if every cost was displayed behind glass with clearly articulated goals to achieve cost reduction, everyone would take the matter seriously. This is the ultimate sharing of critical information in a workplace. Moreover, companies should disclose any information related to their business conditions to their workers so that solutions for solving problems will be automatically generated from concerned workers.

DON'T PLAN WITH NUMBERS FROM THE PAST
OTHERWISE THE SAME WASTES WILL BE INHERITED

HOW COULD YOU BASE YOUR FUTURE PLANNING OFF OF PAST RESULTS?

In the early 60's, Mr. B was working as an administrative operator for Toyota's production management department. Since becoming his superior, Ohno's thinking and attitude had greatly influenced Mr. B. At that time, Ohno was assigned the role of Factory Leader for both the headquarter factory and the Kamigo Factory in Toyota City, Nagoya. He was also a managing director for Toyota. Even though Ohno had been known as "God of the shop floor," the administrative department including, Mr. B, underestimated the fact that Ohno could ever have influenced the way their job was done, even though they had experienced many encounters where their common administrative processes had been completely overturned by Ohno.

For example, a task was given to analyze the level of production efficiency for certain machinery on the shop floor. By calculating the capacity and handling of machinery, when production was to be increased the production management department was able to determine how much production needed to be outsourced with great accuracy. This task was considered to be the most important step in their operation.

After a tremendous amount of effort, they submitted their final report to Ohno. However, he did not intend to read it at all and instead he simply threw it away.

"I am so disappointed in all of you. You can only do wrong calculations," Ohno admonished.

"How can the performance records of the past be used to determine future performance?" Ohno asked the team and turned them away by saying, "If you have time to spare like this you should step onto the shop floor and study it."

Every member in the administrative department, including managers and directors, were completely lost as to how to interpret what Ohno had said. What was more puzzling to them was that the shop floor was able to maintain its calmness despite the fact that they would typically experience chaos when the administrative department became completely lost.

In another case, when a branch factory submitted a request to production management to have a portion of their production outsourced, due to the lack of their production performance, such a request was usually accepted as long it was found to be sound and feasible. However, Ohno no longer accepted such requests, which was later withdrawn by the factory manager. The production management team thought that the request was reasonable enough and that the factory would fail completely if their production could not be outsourced. Instead the factory managed to overcome the hardship without any adverse effects.

Mr. B wondered why the factory did not fail and asked the factory manager,

"How did you manage to survive the situation?"

"Since our request was denied by Ohno we immediately thought about another way by which our production could be contained. We made various continuous improvements and figured out a way to pull it off without any outsourcing," the factory manager replied.

"If it was manageable enough, why did you submit the request in the first place?" Mr. B replied in an unsatisfied manner.

Ohno told Mr. B later, "It is your department's fault that factories often make such requests to ask for help from outsiders. Also, since such requests are always accepted, the factories cease to overcome their own problems by continuous improvement. Your department may be trying their best to help troubled factories, but you are destroying opportunities for those factories to seek continuous improvement for the benefit of their own shop floors."

Mr. B was also told by Kikuo Suzumura, a good friend of mine and the first apprentice of Ohno, "If you do your job, it adds cost to your company. The best thing that could happen to your company is for you to do nothing."

Mr. B felt that everything he had worked for was rejected at once. In the past, the final decision as to whether or not production should be outsourced was always made by him. He had spent so much time collecting scientific information and carrying out complex calculations in order to determine the cost of outsourcing, so that he could make sure that every decision was made effectively. However, Ohno called such information "death certificates."

His information was not only not useful but destroyed every opportunity for factories to implement continuous improvements on their own. Factories were most likely to have a very hard time when their requests were rejected. Ohno strongly believed that humans were able to utilize their intelligence more often in difficult situations, and succeed in generating effective continuous improvement ideas to overcome challenges.

STOP WRITING "DEATH CERTIFICATES"

As Ohno's strategies continued to become rooted in production, the number of requests made by factories for outsourcing production dramatically reduced. In addition, the amount of work that needed to be performed in the administrative department was also diminished.

A few months later Ohno created a continuous improvement team within the production management department, where Mr. B was assigned to continue his work. The team conducted various continuous improvement activities under the guidance of Ohno. The team was referred to as the "Production Inspection Lab," which is still present in Toyota factories today. By the way, I am going to tell you the big secret of this story. Mr. B is Fujio Cho, the current president of Toyota Motors.

I believe that administrative duties should be alleviated by the advancement of information technology but instead I often come across distressed factory managers, who complain about the lack of time they have to step onto the shop floor. Apparently, they are required by higher management to process a high volume of paperwork, for which they spend most of their time in front of their computers. I often ask if such paper work is really necessary. If workers were assigned to produce data that nobody would ever utilize again, the time spent for preparing such data would be the biggest waste of all.

When I would do some paperwork on my desk in the early part of my career, my superior used to tell me, "You can take that paperwork home, but you cannot bring the shop floor with you." This experience taught me the importance of conducting continuous improvement at the actual place, the shop floor. Therefore, I often advise people to ask themselves this question, "Which is more effective to make progress, doing paperwork in the office or formulating solutions on the shop floor?"

I am not suggesting that collecting data or doing paperwork is always wasteful, however if you are being kept away from the shop floor because of it, it would be like concentrating on circumstances at the expense of the main issue. We must start focusing our attention on eliminating the wasteful time spent by asking questions repeatedly like, "Are these documents really necessary?" and "What should be done now?"

REASONING BEHIND THE TOYOTA SYSTEM

Generally speaking, our future planning is often based on historical data. However, Ohno conveyed that historical data inherits various wastes that can be passed on to our new decisions. Therefore, we must refrain from building our decisions upon historical data to avoid the same wastes and flaws our decisions made in the past. The Toyota System believes that continuous improvement in the actual place is the only effective method to eliminate our reliance on historical data.

MEASURE YOUR PERFORMANCE BY PRODUCTIVITY, NOT BY HOW BUSY YOU ARE

DO REAL WORK FOR AT LEAST ONE HOUR PER DAY

In 1946, Ohno gathered up young workers on the shop floor without notice and told them the following,

> "Fellow workers, I urge you to do real work for at least one hour a day. Your work is so wasteful. Show your ideas and stop being so wasteful just for one hour. "

This kind of a remark made every worker feel offended and utter words of rebelliousness. Workers said to one another,

> "He must be joking. We are doing the best we can and even work overtime. What did he mean by "doing real work for at least one hour"?"

Some workers showed a bit of hostility against Ohno. Workers thought that they were trusted by Ohno and felt that the trust was broken for no reason. Their reaction was totally understandable, as they frequently had to work an average of 9 to 10 hours of overtime in a row. Ohno must have known this fact, as he was the managing director of the factory. Being their superior made him realize that their work was being performed in a wasteful manner.

In an example of punching holes in metal rods, a young worker processed 80 rods manually in one day.

> "Why are you punching holes by manual feeding when you have automated machines to do the same job?" Ohno ask the young worker.

> "It is because I can process it faster in this way than automatic feeding," The young worker replied.

Admittedly, the automation required 40 seconds to process one rod, whereas processing by hand only took 30 seconds. However, Ohno kept on questioning the young worker.

> "If one rod takes 30 seconds, 2 rods can be processed in one minute. That means that 120 rods can be processed in one hour, correct?" Ohno asked.

The young worker found himself at a loss for words because he had thought that he was doing his best by processing only 80 rods in one day.

> "According to my calculation you should be processing 80 rods within 40 minutes, meaning that you are putting in real work for only 40 minutes per day. I am sure that you are trying your best but your performance is not acceptable. Do me a favor and perform real work at least one hour per day," Ohno said to the young worker, with a gentle tone in his voice.

The reasons why the young worker took 8 hours to process 80 rods are as follows:

(1) Manual Feeding

It takes 30 seconds to process one component by manual feeding. However, the tip of the drill gets overheated after 3 components are processed consecutively and must be sharpened frequently. Workers have to wait in line to sharpen the drill, as the number of grinders available on the shop floor is limited. Grinding of the drill takes only 30 seconds, however the whole process usually takes 10 minutes if you include the trip to and from the grinders.

(2) Automatic Feeding

In contrast, it takes 40 seconds to process one component by automatic feeding. The drill automatically turns off before it gets overheated, therefore there is no need for grinding the drill. All workers have to do is set the components to be fed into the machine and let it run automatically while they continue to perform other tasks.

REMOVE WASTES FROM WORK ITSELF

Ohno often emphasized that various wastes existed in the way we had always conducted our work. He always helped his workers to realize this, which led to an increase in their productivity. Ohno may have used a harsh way of telling them to do real work at least for an hour a day, but he was only hoping to motivate workers.

There is actually a good reason behind Ohno's method, who had taken such a harsh attitude toward his workers since the 1940's, when World War II had finally come to an end. The year the war was over, Kiichiro Toyoda, the founder of Toyota Motors, gave a pep talk to his company workers.

"We must catch up with American auto–makers within three years, otherwise the Japanese automobile industry will be bound to fail completely."

In those days, productivity of Japanese industry was only $1/8^{th}$ of that of American industry. Ohno determined the productivity of Japanese workers had to be increased by 8 times. However, he never thought that Japanese workers would have to work 8 times as hard as American workers, nor that Americans were working harder than Japanese workers. He thought that the difference in productivity could be explained by the fact that Japanese workers were being more wasteful in production. Therefore, Japanese industries could manage to exceed American industries by completely eliminating wastes from production.

With this in mind, Ohno looked carefully at the shop floor and not to his surprise, observed various wastes. There were many cases where workers would waste 8 hours of labor and perform real work for only 40 minutes to yield a true added-value to production. Ohno's strong belief was that production could be boosted by 8 times once each worker learned to perform waste-free work for 8 hours, even if they had to start doing so by performing productive work for only 1 hour per day. This was the starting point of Ohno's principle, "Working with Human Intelligence."

In the beginning, Ohno's request to perform actual work for at lease one hour each day was accepted with resistance among the workers. Most workers already tried their best and often received compliments for their devotion from their supervisors. It was understandable that they became offended when they were told by Ohno to do real work for at least one hour.

As a matter of fact, Ohno intended this to be as sort of shock treatment. With his shocking remarks and persistent effort of getting workers to visualize wastes in production, Ohno attempted to convey the true purpose behind his behaviors.

REASONING BEHIND THE TOYOTA SYSTEM

Toyota believes that true efficiency can be gained by continuous progress within processes and not by how hard workers are doing their jobs. How many hours can you say that you are doing real work inside your working hours? I am aware that things have changed dramatically since the time the Toyota System was created, however we must remember that true efficiency is gained by continuous progress within processes at any given time.

PRODUCE ONLY NECESSARY ITEMS

OVERPRODUCTION LEADS TO WASTES

What is the biggest difference between the Toyota Production System and Mass Production?

Sellers' Mkt.

Mass Production—Sales forecasts determine the intensity of production. Production takes place under an assumption that every item can be sold in the future, even if they remain in inventory for a while.

Buyers' Mkt

Toyota Production System—Market demand is carefully analyzed and only the necessary items are produced in the necessary quantity. Overproduction due to inaccurate sales forecasts is considered to be one of the biggest wastes in production.

After reading that, it is easier to understand how wasteful it is to produce items that are neither saleable, nor necessary. However, back in the time of the industrial revolution, when mass production was standardized on the shop floor, it was extremely challenging for factories to grasp the new concept. As I remember, Ohno often told managers of the shop floors,

> "Materials such as steel sheets and threads do not make your stomach full."

Let me explain what he meant by that. Many of Toyota's retirees built their own factories with their retirement money and Toyota often used their factories. The retirees were–without a doubt–experienced and skilled engineers, however they were lacking serious management skills. They manufactured the best products they could produce but failed to produce items that were demanded by the market. This was the main reason why their factories were managed by more experienced managers, even though they owned the factories.

> Ohno used to say, "If you don't know how to manage your own factories, you will soon become an employee of your own factory. Look at your factory carefully. Workers are working hard to produce all this stuff, but remember Toyota only purchases what is necessary. Even when you spend all the labor and time to produce the best steel component possible, it could easily become a waste if Toyota decided not to purchase it. That means that you will not get any money to pay for the production costs, such as electricity and press machines.
>
> "What is left is a block of useless steel. How would you feed your wife and children if you were the owner of this factory? You probably don't know what I am talking about here because you are receiving salary. But if you were the owner, you would be licking the steel. What's worse is that if you owned a textile factory you would be licking threads... and that has no taste at all!"

With his unique sense of humor, Ohno continued to convey to his workers the importance of removing wasteful work-in-progress items and excess inventories.

INVENTORY IS A CRIME

The basic principle in manufacturing is to analyze market demand carefully and base production on that. In the past, a high economic growth period various commodities were scarce, therefore every product was sold easily because of the high demands among consumers. Having stock was a common practice back then as it was only a short matter of time before products were cleared out of inventories.

Large machinery was purchased for production to keep up with the market demands. Workers did not even take into consideration any sales needs or market demands, all they needed to focus on was manufacturing a wide range of products, as many and as quickly as possible. Factories had operated under these circumstances for many years and mass production had become the main process taught to the shop floor workers.

During that same time period Toyota Motors had started to take a different approach to production. Their approach was, fundamentally, to "produce only saleable items." Toyota learned that very important lesson when it faced bankruptcy in 1950, due to holding a large volume of inventories. In other words, the Japanese automobile industry, in the post-war period, became financially vulnerable and could not afford to maintain inventories in order to complete with well-established companies overseas.

What did Ohno mean by "necessary items?" It basically means a "sales trend." Everything is determined by the market demand. The necessary items are decided by the market and should not be controlled by decisions made only on the shop floor. The real challenge here is to produce the necessary items at the lowest cost possible. It is referred to as "Limited Amount Management," or limiting both the cost and quantity of production. This is what separates it from the "Make to Stock" production system.

The "Make to Stock" production system is simply based on assumptions and the sales forecasts of producers. However, such assumptions are often inaccurate, which causes factories to suffer from excessive inventories. Even with elaborate sales forecasts, which are made by carefully analyzing the market, it is not that simple to predict the market as business climates and people's hobbies change quite unexpectedly. Another disadvantage of the "Make to Stock" production system is a failure to meet the market demand when it exceeds the volume of production. This also means a loss of opportunity to sell more items on the market.

The Toyota System clearly understands that their production systems must accommodate gradual changes in the market demand and allow a flexible production mechanism in order to facilitate efficient transitions for both an increase and decrease in production. In order to systemize such a production system, the shop floor management had to associate a sense of guilt with holding inventories and to keep firmly in mind, at all times, that only saleable items needed to be produced.

REASONING BEHIND THE TOYOTA SYSTEM

It is considered wasteful to:

- Produce items that are assumed to sell

- Produce items in less time than needed

- Produce more items than needed

Over-production, especially, can lead to various wastes other than maintaining inventories, such as an increase in In-Process Stock (increased holding time due to material shortages or process delays), waste of movement, and waste of transportation. True work lies in a production system where only the necessary items are produced in the necessary quantity at the right time. The Toyota System calls it "Just-In-Time."

Commandment 2

*"Hang in there and never give up once you begin,
otherwise you will make it a habit to leave
things unfinished."*

DISCOVER THE TRUTH BEYOND YOUR UNDERSTANDING

STAND AND OBSERVE THE SHOP FLOOR

A young Toyota worker, Mr. C, was taking a break after having finished a continuous improvement activity on the shop floor. Ohno approached Mr. C and was told that the continuous improvement was successfully achieved. Without uttering a word, Ohno studied the shop floor where Mr. C supposedly had applied continuous improvement.

Ohno pointed his finger at the floor and said to Mr. C, "Draw a circle here with chalk."

Mr. C was confused but did what he was told to do, and drew a small circle on the floor.

"You idiot! How are you going to stand in such a small circle?" Ohno asked.

Mr. C redrew a bigger circle and was ordered by Ohno to stand in the circle and observe the shop floor for a while. Mr. C had no clue as to what this was all about, but he could not object to Ohno and decided to stand in the circle as told.

Around lunch time Mr. C heard nature calling, so he stepped out of the circle to use the bathroom. When he returned to the circle Ohno was standing by it to see what had happened.

> "Why did you step out of the circle without permission?" Ohno asked.
>
> "Well, I needed to use the bathroom pretty badly," Mr. C began.
>
> "After you have lunch come back to this circle and stand in it. If you need to leave the circle for any reason, you must get permission," Ohno gave his instructions to Mr. C and left the scene.

Mr. C simply had no choice so he stood in the circle. He did not know what to look for and just observed the shop floor without any purpose.

> In the early evening Ohno came back and asked Mr. C, "So, have you figured it out yet?"
>
> "I just have no idea," Mr. C answered honestly.
>
> Ohno gathered his thoughts and said, "I see. You can go home now, but you will need to stand here tomorrow morning as well."

Mr. C almost brought himself to ask Ohno what this was all about but he knew, as always, that Ohno would ask him to figure out the answer to his own question.

He returned and stood in the circle the next morning. He

was smart enough to know that he needed to be looking for some problems, since Ohno had personally ordered him to observe the shop floor, but he could not figure out what the problem was, much less what he was supposed to be doing about it.

Ohno came to see him around lunch time and asked, "Have you figured this out yet?"

"Yes. There is a problem," Mr. C answered with uncertainty hoping to put an end to the whole situation.

Ohno did not ask him what he discovered, but instead pointed a finger at the shop floor and said, "Observe how the shop floor workers conduct their operations. You told me that you had continuously improved the shop floor but it has gotten worse because of your instructions! If you know what the real problem is now, go and fix it right away."

He looked at the shop floor again and agreed that workers were still having a hard time doing their duties. He immediately interviewed the shop floor workers and formulated another continuous improvement strategy to remedy the issues.

The problem was that he automatically assumed that his initial continuous activity had been successful and did not carefully confirm its results. Ohno knew immediately that the problems that still existed on the shop floor; instead of telling Mr. C right away, Ohno wanted to teach him a lesson in his unique way of ordering his workers to stand in a circle.

Ohno focused on teaching workers two things:

(1) Observe the shop floor closely.

(2) See through a continuous improvement activity and confirm the positive results with your own eyes.

It took as long as one and a half days for Mr. C to learn the lesson but this experience had opened his eyes and enabled him to approach the shop floor with a greater level of accuracy and confidence throughout his career.

HOW CAN YOU BASE YOUR FUTURE PLANNING ON PAST RESULTS?

> Once, when Ohno was touring a company, he asked the factory tour guide, "How much time does this process take?"
>
> "I think it is around 15 minutes," the tour guide answered, without knowing anything for sure.

Without moving at all Ohno continue to observe the shop floor workers in detail. He counted down the time and the process did not get completed within the 15 minutes.

> "I knew it. It took more than the time you specified. This is because your workers are doing their jobs in a wasteful manner. You must fix the problem by continuous improvement right away," Ohno told the management personnel and continued touring the factory.

As Ohno emphasized all the time, if there is a problem the true cause of it must be identified by observing each process carefully. At the same time, the existing issues and assumptions must be confirmed by stepping onto the shop floor and determining their accuracy. *Both the starting and ending points of true work reside on the shop floor.*

I personally have had similar experiences with Ohno. When I told him that a certain continuous improvement activity was carried out on the shop floor he often asked me if I had seen any positive results because of it or not.

There is a famous episode with the founder of the Toyota Group, Sakichi Toyoda, in which he would spend all day observing some elderly females weaving in the neighborhood while he was inventing the automatic loom. Ohno was simply the same way. Continuous improvement requires a perfect comprehension of the shop floor and to accomplish that Ohno repeatedly told his workers,

> "Stand in the shop floor and observe the processes all day long. You will come to understand what must be done to resolve the most critical problems."

REASONING BEHIND THE TOYOTA SYSTEM

It is easy to say "Observe the shop floor" or "Know the shop floor," however it is always challenging to discover the true problem and figure out an effective continuous improvement solution simply by our observation. When you think that you have figured it all out, your decisions are still often limited to the scope your own knowledge. Therefore, continuous improvement solutions created in this manner often fail to succeed.

You will begin to establish the most effective solution by persistently searching for truths and observing every process on the shop floor repeatedly until the real issues are discovered. The Toyota System has strongly encouraged this self-training process among their workers in order to promote the most effective problem-solving skills.

AVOID FIRST-AID REMEDIES; DEVELOP A HABIT OF ANALYZING PROBLEMS THOROUGHLY ON THE SHOP FLOOR

DID YOU APPLY AN APPROPRIATE SOLUTION?

A Toyota worker, Mr. D, had worked for Toyota for 5 years when he was assigned to work on a project that was designed to increase manufacturing productivity for newly released cars. While working on this project he had an opportunity to meet Ohno for the very first time. Mr. D had heard about Ohno's unique personality and leadership, however it was not until he actually worked with Ohno that he was truly astonished by Ohno's passion and dedication toward continuous improvement.

Mr. D was instructed by Ohno to provide a component supplier with training for their Kanban System (a mechanism used to instruct the production and transportation of items.) The supplier was suffering from the loss of Kanbans in the course of their production process. The basic rule is that production stops unless a physical Kanban comes in to order more. By this method wasteful production can be eliminated, as long as this rule is strictly adhered to.

The problem was that physical Kanbans were lost and never reached the shop floor to initiate the production process. If the shop floor followed the rule then production would not take place, in spite of the actual orders, which created various problems for their own company as well as their customers, such as Toyota. Mr. D decided to provide a first-aid solution to the problem by increasing the number of Kanbans.

This was quite a risky solution. If the missing Kanbans were later discovered then the shop floor would produce the quantity instructed by them as well, causing a rapid increase in the existing inventory. However, to Mr. D, as inexperienced as he was, it was more important to meet the deadline than deal with the risk of double-production. Ohno learned about the incident and became enraged.

> "You did not even attempt to look for the missing Kanbans and decided to replace them with new ones without permission. Go back to the shop floor and find those missing Kanbans immediately!"

> Mr. D was intimidated by Ohno's furious behavior and spent more than one hour searching for the missing Kanbans. He had absolutely no luck and told Ohno, "I looked everywhere for the missing Kanbans, but I could not find them."

> Ohno replied, with the same level of intensity as before, "What do you mean by you looked

everywhere? You only spent one hour of your time!"

He went back to look for them more carefully but still had no luck. He thought that the Kanbans were not to be found, given how many hours were spent looking for them, and that Ohno would understand that as well.

> He reported back to Ohno and told him, "I spent many more hours looking for the missing Kanbans. I am sorry to tell you that I could not find them anywhere."

> "Do you know why you cannot find the missing Kanbans no matter how hard you try?" Ohno asked.

> Mr. D did not know how to answer the question and was told by Ohno, "It is simple. You do not have an intention to keep searching until you can find them."

Mr. D found himself becoming more serious than he thought he could become about the missing Kanbans. He traced back his search routes and continued to visit places he would have never considered in his desperate attempt to locate the Kanbans. It was when he almost decided to give up again that he finally located them by subconsciously lifting up a component box. The missing Kanbans were stuck on the bottom of the component boxes as they were stacked. As a result all of the missing Kanbans were fully recovered and Mr. D could not wait to tell Ohno about it.

> He told Ohno with joy, "I found them finally!"

> Much to his disappointment Ohno did not reply with, "I am so proud that you found them," instead he simply replied, "Have you already implemented a solution for that?"

REPEAT "WHY?" FIVE TIMES

The assignment given to Mr. D was not simply to locate the missing Kanbans. He was supposed to analyze the true cause of the problem and facilitate a continuous improvement solution so that the same mistake would not be repeated ever again on the shop floor.

Mr. D found that Kanbans had been attached to the top of the component boxes and were pasted, by accident, onto the oily bottoms of other boxes as they were stacked. To solve this problem, Mr. D instructed that Kanbans should be attached on the side of the component boxes, which successfully eliminated the issue of missing Kanbans. After this incident the supplier became proficient in utilizing Kanbans in their operations.

Mr. D came to understand that first-aid solutions should never be applied and instead an analysis of the true cause of a problem is absolutely necessary so that effective solutions can be put into practice. He also acknowledged that 2 important lessons had been taught by Ohno:

(1) Implacability in asking yourself "Why?" five times.

It is easy to simply instruct people to repeat "Why?" five times. However, as in the case of Mr. D, a tremendous effort and devotion is often necessary to draw answers for the first "Why?" Many of my colleagues from Toyota had experiences of being instructed by Ohno to discover the true cause of problems over the period of several days, or even that of many months. In some cases, asking "Why?" needed to be repeated six or seven times until the true cause was discovered. Solutions formulated after asking "Why?" only two or three times are not the real solutions, as the true cause has yet to be found. In this case, the same problems are often repeated and lead to more serious consequences.

(2) Fix it at the core instead of just patching it.

Ohno taught me the difference between "fixing" the problem and "patching" (first-aid) the problem. When a machine breaks down it may require some first-aid repairs, such as replacing parts. However, the machine is most likely going to break down again, as the true cause of the problem was never fixed at the core. This is just "patching" the problem and is not "fixing" the problem. "Fixing" seeks out the true cause of a problem and removes it so that the same mistake is never repeated. "Fixing" is one of the most important practices in Toyota. Toyota also applies this practice beyond machineries to many other sorts of problems so that a strong-minded shop floor is established in the end.

REASONING BEHIND THE TOYOTA SYSTEM

The Toyota System requires "Why?" to be repeated until true causes are discovered. It is indeed a tough challenge for everyone, but our work requires a strong commitment to overcome problems if it is to be meaningful at all. In other words, a new array of work becomes apparent to us as the result of our devotion to the existing work.

DON'T JUST DO WHAT YOU CAN, DO UNTIL YOU CAN

SEARCH FOR THE ANSWER UNTIL YOU FIND IT

In the world of quality control it was often considered acceptable to find three defects in 1,000 products. That is a defect rate of only 0.3%. This could easily pass the quality control standards of the past, however it is simply unthinkable by today's quality standards. Despite the fact that such an allowable defect rate has been improved over the years, many factories still believe that a certain percentage of their production is inevitably going to become defects in one form or another. As I described previously, Ohno strongly believed that defects could be reduced to absolute zero with no exceptions.

Mr. E was a technical instructor who worked on the assembly line for the factory managed by Ohno. He was in charge of attaching clamps and screw nuts onto the body frames in the automobile section. One day, a frame advanced to the post process without a necessary clamp attached completely to it, and was later returned back to Mr. E. Ohno happened to step into the shop floor and found this defective frame was being kept on the floor.

> He immediately called for Mr. E and asked, "What in the world is this all about?"
>
> "It was retuned by the post process because it was missing the clamp on it," Mr. E replied.
>
> "Have you learned where and why it was detached from the frame?" Ohno asked.
>
> "I have no clue," Mr. E replied.
>
> "Shame on you! It is the most important aspect of your work. Investigate this case until you are absolutely sure how this happened," Ohno fumed.

It was his first time being reprimanded by Ohno with such intensity. Because of his experiences in working as a technical instructor he knew the significance of inspecting reasons why the defect came about in the first place. However, he had wished that this would be an exception due to its rare occurrence. He knew that rarity, and the many possible causing factors, were just too large a problem to manage on his own and he did not like to push disruptions onto other departments. He also knew that Ohno would never accept this as an exception since the problem had come to the surface in the first place.

Mr. E started his investigation as ordered by Ohno,

though he knew it was going to be extremely difficult. In order to find defects he had to observe the "scene of the crime" of the defect at the time it was produced. Since the reoccurrence rate was so low he thought it was simply impossible to witness the same defect occur again. Mr. E persistently looked for the defect for over two days with no luck at all.

He reported to Ohno hoping that he would be ordered to stop searching.

> "I spent the last two days looking for it, but nothing could be found."

> "Keep on looking until you find it," Ohno simply replied.

On the third day, he witnessed the moment when the clamp snapped off in the engineering shop. It was outside his jurisdiction so he called the manager in charge and instructed him to implement a continuous improvement measure to eliminate the problem.

As ordered by Ohno, he spent three straight days investigating the cause and successfully overcame what had been considered impossible. If he had simply given up, this could never have been achieved.

NEVER ACCEPT EXCEPTIONS

I was often told by Ohno that exceptions such as three defects out of 1,000 products should be cherished as they always indicate room for more improvements. By eliminating exceptions one by one, the zero-defect goal becomes more attainable while at the same time improving the quality of overall production.

Toyota's quality control tactics have deep roots in the development of automated weaving machines by Sakichi Toyoda. Sakichi's weaving machines were equipped with safety devices that allowed stopping of the machines when threads snapped or ran out, for instance. This mechanism successfully eliminated even the slightest chance for any defects to be formed. Strong determination for "zero-de-fect control" was launched from this time onward.

Ohno strongly believed that zero-defect control could be accomplished by implementing this mechanism not only to machinery but also to processes performed by humans. Every machine detects abnormalities and is given a capacity to automatically shut itself down. In the same manner, each worker is capable of stopping the entire production line if he detects irregularities in one form or another. This is called "Automation with a Human Touch," which allowed the realization of a defect-free production mechanism, after effective continuous improvement measures are implemented to remedy the true cause of a problem.

If defects still managed to occur Ohno did not simply exclude them as rare exceptions. Instead spent a great deal of effort in encouraging his workers to eliminate such defects, even the their occurrence rate was close to 1/10,000 or even 1/100,000.

The current president of Toyota Motors, Fujio Cho, shared his experience with Ohno.

> "In the past it was considered an exception in the industry to see 3 defects in every 1,000 products. Ohno, on the other hand, used to tell me, "Are you a novice? You must take it much more seriously if as many as 3 defects occur in every 1,000 items. That's a lot of defects." We would produce only 100 items per day, so that meant defects could occur once every 3 production days.

> "Our real challenge, which came later, was how we could possibly track down a defect if it only occurred once in every 10,000 items. Ohno did not think this to be an exception either. He would tell me to keep standing on the shop floor until I could see it. His reasoning was that the occurrence of a defect was like physics; if the same conditions are met, it is bound to happen again. So, I would just keep standing until

I finally found it."

REASONING BEHIND THE TOYOTA SYSTEM

The elimination of defects is a never-ending goal in the field of manufacturing. This goal can never be achieved if even the slightest percentage of defects are viewed as exceptions. A strong determination for our "zero-defect goal" must be present and we must dedicate ourselves to observing the shop floor for a number of days until we can witness the crime. It sounds extremely challenging to accomplish, however you must try until you pull it off. That is the Toyota way.

DON'T BECOME CONCEITED BY BEING SATISFIED WITH IMMEDIATE RESULTS; AVOID BEING OVERCONFIDENT

FORGET ABOUT WHAT HAPPENED YESTERDAY

The most difficult stage in a continuous improvement activity is when positive results begin to appear on the surface. "Everything we could possibly do was done. Nothing more can be continuously improved at this point." Such a self-conceited attitude should be eliminated. One must reset oneself and go back to their first objective so that new motivation towards continuous improvement can be attained.

The reward is usually huge and easy to see during the beginning stages of implementing continuous improvement measures. Positive results are easily achievable and enjoyable by even rough measures at first. This is more true if continuous improvement activities are initiated in a more wasteful production environment. Our challenge remains, after acquiring the first set of objectives (by carrying out only the most basic continuous improvement), to define the next set of goals and overcome the tendency to be satisfied with only the easily-attainable goals.

A widely-improved shop floor often says, "We have done great work so far. We have nothing left to improve."

This is a sign of over-satisfaction.

Toyota worker Mr. F performed a series of continuous improvements in the production line, which enabled performing a certain process by only three workers, instead of five. As a result, the production cost was reduced dramatically and Mr. F received many compliments from his colleagues. He himself thought it was a wonderful job and felt overly satisfied with the end result.

> Ohno told Mr. F, "Think beyond that. What comes after reducing the number of workers?"

Mr. F had no idea what Ohno meant at first. He honestly thought there was nothing more to be done after eliminating two workers. The result was good enough and no other department had been as successful in reducing the number of workers as drastically as he had.

> "There is nothing more that can be improved from this," he told Ohno.

> "Improve further what you have already continuously improved. That is what separates true professionals from average workers," Ohno replied.

Ohno strongly believed that only death can separate continuous improvement from a worker. When one sprout of waste is removed another sprout grows immediately in its place. Workers must always think beyond their achievement and should not remain satisfied with what was already accomplished in the past or they would miss a new sprout of waste.

Ohno once told me an analogy to explain the dangers of self-conceit. He used the story of a student and master of Japanese sword fighting. To become a sword fighter, a student trains under his master in the beginning. After vigorous training the student was able to win one game out of three from his respected master. If he thinks and feels satisfied here, "I can win one game out of three against my master therefore there is nothing more for me to learn," he ceases to improve himself beyond this point.

For those who become true masters, they will focus on nurturing their intelligence at this point. They may meditate or isolate themselves in the mountains to reflect on their past knowledge and experiences so that they could become free from all distracting thoughts. By doing so, ones moral character and a higher level of intelligence are formed, reaching the realm of a sword fighting master.

Ohno thought that feeling satisfied with your own continuous improvement was like being content with winning only one game of sword fighting out of 3, and that such workers would be limiting their own potential to grow. To promote this idea on a daily basis, Ohno often said,

> "Forget about what you accomplished yesterday. Do not think about tomorrow either. Something is wrong and wasteful with what you are doing now and today. There is still room for continuous improvement as we speak."

With this recommendation in mind, Ohno guided his workers through continuous improvement on a regular basis.

ONCE THE GOAL IS REACHED, REPLACE IT WITH A NEW ONE

Mr. F started to think differently after the incident with Ohno.

> "No matter how hard I work to get the results I desire, I should not remain satisfied. As a professional, it is extremely important for me to initiate a new challenge on my own in an attempt to seek the ultimate production mechanism by a never-ending continuous improvement effort. "

It is extremely important to feel a sense of triumph in our intellectual development, to a certain degree. However, if it turns into excessive self-satisfaction, humans will cease to grow beyond that, and, in some cases, can even begin to degrade. Self-confidence should be valued but overconfidence should be eliminated.

Stick to it until the end. The secret to success is setting a higher, sometimes unattainable goal. This is what Ohno wanted to convey to all of us. Ohno used to say the following in regards to setting goals,

> "The real goal is to challenge our human intellectual potential without end. A goal must be set even higher immediately after it is reached."

REASONING BEHIND THE TOYOTA SYSTEM

The secret behind the Toyota System lies in its endless benchmarking techniques. Benchmarking promotes a way of growth in which you are compared to the best processes or people and continuously adapt such best practices to achieve progress. While staying hungry for better and cheaper things in the world, a goal must be replaced with a higher goal once it is achieved and continuous improvement must be practiced endlessly to achieve each goal. This perseverance is what has made the top companies that exist in the world today what they are.

Commandment 3

"Keep your workers challenged. This creates an intellectual advantage over those who prefer an easier way."

INCREASING PRODUCTION WHILE LIMITING THE NUMBER OF WORKERS IS THE ONLY WAY TO GAIN TRUE SUCCESS

GIVING EVERYONE A HARD TIME IS YOUR RESPONSIBILITY

The following story took place in the first half of 1965 when the Toyota Corolla was selling extremely well. Ohno gave instructions to the production manager for the engine processing department.

"Produce 5,000 engines with less than 100 workers," Ohno ordered.

The production manager reported back to Ohno a few months later and said, "We are now able to produce 5,000 engines with only

80 workers."

The sale of Corolla's continued to rise, however, requiring the production to be increased accordingly. Ohno asked a question.

"How many workers do you think are needed to produce 10,000 engines?"

"160 workers would be sufficient," the production manager replied.

This answer infuriated Ohno. "I learned how to figure out 8 x 2 = 16 in elementary school. I had never thought I would learn that again from you when I am this old. Do not treat me like a fool."

The production manager had no intention whatsoever of insulting Ohno, he just gave a simple answer. His logic was that if 80 workers were needed to produce 5,000 engines, it would require twice as many workers to complete 10,000 engines. It was so obvious to him.

However, Ohno never allowed this kind of an answer, as it was to so amateur and lacking intelligence.

Ohno added, "You are so accustomed to a notion that any form of increase in sales, labor and equipment is considered favorable. But, how do you ensure that our profit keeps on increasing? That is the most critical factor."

In other words, business should not be operated based merely on the management of arithmetic, such as 8 x 2 = 16 in this scenario. When production needs to be doubled we must apply our intelligence and creativity in order to establish the most effective continuous improvement measures so that we can limit the labor cost and maximize our profit. Ohno called it "Management by Ninja Art." Based on this reason, Ohno scolded the production manager for simply doubling the number of workers without putting any creative thinking into it.

After this incident, the production manager carried out a wide range of continuous improvement strategies and succeeded in reducing the number of required workers to only 100. He pulled this off by shifting away from simple arithmetic solving, as instructed by Ohno.

To give you another example, say 100 workers are required to produce 5,000 engines. Sales remain strong and 6,000 engines are soon needed to be prepared. What would Ohno do in this case? His idea would be, "Increase production without increasing workers." Ohno did not encourage any labor enforcement, where workers were given unreasonable deadlines, instead he expected his workers to apply their intelligence and repeat continuous improvement so that even what was considered to be an impossible goal became achievable.

Say the goal was achieved after hard work and production was ordered to level down to 5,000 engines. Typically, it would be a big relief for workers and they may decide not to work as hard anymore. However, Ohno would push them one step further and give them a hard time. Ohno would give an order like,

> "We were using 100 workers to produce 6,000 engines in this production line. Reduce the number of workers to LESS than 100 to produce 5,000 engines since the production was ordered to be reduced."

This would be an extremely difficult challenge for workers. It is true that 100 workers did manage to produce 6,000 engines by vigorous continuous improvement ideas, however completing 5,000 engines has always needed a bare minimum of 100 workers. Ohno did not care about the fact that 100 workers was the requirement for completing 5,000 engines because that was only true prior to continuous improvement.

Reducing the number of workers is a common practice to limit the production cost while securing productivity. The only challenge here was to find solutions to make efficient adjustments with available resources, or less, as the production output changed.

Ohno also made it a habit to say,

"It is my job to give everyone a hard time."

By doing so, Ohno trained his workers to challenge impossible goals and gain continuous improvement skills by applying their intelligence and experiences to problem solving. It is a fact that Ohno's approach has lead to Toyota's competitive edge over other companies over the many years that followed.

BIG REASONS WHY TOYOTA HAS BECOME SO SUCCESSFUL

The Toyota System has been all about seeking innovative solutions for accommodating the increasing volume of orders while minimizing the number of workers. In 1950, Toyota Motors faced the risk of bankruptcy and overcame it by being financed by a new set of bank loans in exchange for eliminating close to 2,000 employees, as well as the resignation from the original founder, Kiichiro Toyoda. This was when Toyota learned the risk of producing items based solely on sales assumptions and reduced their monthly production output down from 1,000 cars to 800.

When the Korean War broke out unexpectedly, soon after Toyota faced their financial crisis, Toyota received a large volume of orders for supplying trucks for the war. Ishida Taizo was the president at the time and was responsible for restoring the financial state of Toyota. He did not allow the number of workers to be increased and instead provided solutions to accommodate the increasing orders with the available resources. It would have been simply impossible to overcome this challenge if the old way of production had been used. The creative minds of Eiji Toyoda and Ohno lead to the establishment of an innovative production system that helped Toyota survive the crisis.

I remember Ohno saying repeatedly that he could not sleep some nights because he was brainstorming for new ideas. He also told me that the fact Toyota was able to boost production without increasing workers has made Toyota what it is today. In other words, when Toyota was faced with limited resources, such as labor, equipment, investment and raw materials, Toyota chose to utilize human intelligence to draw effective solutions to enhance productivity. This was the starting point in the development of the Toyota Production System.

REASONING BEHIND THE TOYOTA SYSTEM

There is nothing challenging about manufacturing when abundant amounts of resources, such as workers, equipment, raw materials, and financial investment, are available. On the other hand, if such resources are scarce it is an entirely different story, as you can expect. Only in these types of situations do humans learn to utilize their intelligence to come up with solutions. The most effective allocations of labor and equipment are carefully analyzed so that wastes and defects are completely removed from production. Even when resources were abundant, Ohno often pushed his workers over the edge — giving instructions to boost production without increasing workers, so that his workers never ceased to apply their intelligence to improve production.

DON'T SELECT WORK BASED ON WHAT'S POSSIBLE OR NOT, ALWAYS DECIDE BASED ON WHAT'S NECESSARY OR NOT

IMPOSSIBILITY LEADS TO NEW IDEAS

Changeovers of machinery are needed to run from one product to another. In the beginning of 1965, Toyota would spend two to four hours performing a single changeover per 1,000 ton press machine. When a changeover took place the process was put on hold, which made it almost impossible to maintain a high operation rate. This was true especially for Toyota, who focused mainly on high-variety, low volume manufacturing. Therefore, the biggest challenge for Toyota was to minimize the time required to perform changeovers on the shop floor.

Toyota initially set a goal of reducing their changeover time to *less* than two hours. At that time Volkswagon was already performing their changeovers in just two hours and Toyota wanted to beat their competition. With the help of a production engineering consultant, Shingo Shigeo, young engineers used their intelligence to come up with a strategy. Eventually, the changeover time was reduced to only one hour.

There were two kinds of changeovers performed at Toyota back then:

> **(1) Internal Changeover** — Machinery must be stopped to perform a changeover.

> **(2) External Changeover** — A changeover can be performed while machinery is running or after the process is complete.

Each process chose to implement either one of these two changeovers in an ambiguous manner. By clearly distinguishing the applicability of these changeovers, External Changeovers were heavily promoted to all of the suitable processes, and continuous improvement measures were formulated independently on each type of changeover. Six months were spent in doing so and eventually the changeover time was reduced to only one hour, down from four hours, and almost everyone was satisfied with the result. However, Ohno was not satisfied and gave everyone another challenge.

> "Now reduce the changeover time to less than 10 minutes," Ohno bluntly told his workers.

The project team thought there was absolutely no way this was possible and were completely lost as to how to approach this challenge. However, Ohno's orders had to be followed and the changeover time for a 1,000 ton press machine had to be reduced to less than 10 minutes.

What appeared to be an impossible-to-achieve goal not only gives people a hard time, but also motivates humans to fully utilize their intellectual possibilities. The team leader did not give up and felt challenged by the new goal.

The team suggested over a hundred improvement topics and worked exclusively towards turning Internal Changeovers into External Changeovers. A mechanism that allowed a changeover (switching blades and molds, etc) to be completed with a touch of the button was also introduced. Clamps no longer used bolts or could be tightened by turning the bolts only once, which reduced the changeover time in increments of seconds.

The changeover time was finally reduced to seven minutes, and the results were miraculous. The accumulation of small innovative ideas realized the goal. Techniques used in this challenge were also applied to the development of "Single Minute Exchange of Die" that allowed a complete changeover within 10 minutes. The development of "One-Touch Changeover" was also triggered and implemented in many other processes, allowing a changeover to be completed within only seconds.

This achievement signifies a milestone in the development of the Toyota System. The group leader believed that "Single Minute Exchange of Die" would not have been invented if Ohno had not ordered it. The point is that impossible goals can lead us to generate ideas that we never thought we could possibly have.

WHY GIVE UP BEFORE YOU TRY IT?

No one was more delighted with the result than Ohno. Ohno himself was having a hard time eliminating wasteful changeovers and was running out of continuous improvement ideas. The eventual achievement of reducing the changeover time to 3 minutes was extremely critical to many other important future developments of the Toyota System, especially the "One-piece Flow."

In my personal experiences, Ohno often gave me various impossible challenges to overcome when we were absorbed in continuous improvement activities. He would become furious if we simply replied to him by saying, "I cannot do it" or "It is impossible."

> Ohno would say, "How can you think it is impossible if you do not try it at all? You are not a fortune teller."

Ohno gave everybody a hard time without any hesitation, he was natural at that. However, it is doubtful that Ohno always expected the challenges to be realized by his workers. Achievement of SMED was a good example. However, Ohno had always believed that challenges could be overcome in one way or another and conveyed to his workers the importance of trying.

The son of Sakichi Toyoda, Kiichiro, had a tendency to reject possibilities on the basis of the principles he had learned at the university. Sakichi always advised him to at least give it a try. Kiichiro was skeptical at first but decided to give things a try and, to his surprise, he was able to achieve what he had thought to be impossible. Since then he became a true believer in trying instead of drawing conclusions in his head and simply giving up. Ohno was the same way.

For example, we tend to incorporate only a partial improvement to achieve small goals, such as reducing the production cost by 10%. Say we are asked to cut the production cost in half, this often leads us to some revolutionary solutions to achieve such a difficult goal. We may look into overhauling the entire production system or changing the raw materials to be used in production.

Toyota has always cherished their worker's waste-consciousness and ability eliminate even the smallest waste on a regular basis (Waste Removal Continuous Improvement). At the same time, Toyota sets nearly-impossible goals and puts up a good fight toward achieving such goals (Problem Challenge Continuous Improvement).

A good example is that Toyota acquired the famous "CCC21" Achievement (Construction of Cost Competitiveness in the 21st Century) by reducing their production cost by 1 trillion yen over three years. Such an achievement goes back to the very words of Ohno, "Apply SMED to all of our processes. It is never impossible if we try."

REASONING BEHIND THE TOYOTA SYSTEM

If you think you cannot do it before you even try, you may miss some of life's greatest opportunities. When you have a positive attitude you will be surprised at how much is actually possible to achieve. The basic lesson of Toyota is to "always try it first." Work requires two types of people, one throws a ball as far away as possible, and the other gives ideas on how it can be fetched.

LEAD THEM TO AN ANSWER BUT DON'T GIVE IT AWAY

SURPRISING IDEAS COME ABOUT WHEN ONE IS IN DESPAIR

Ohno never explained to his workers the reasons why continuous improvement was necessary, let alone described how it could be achieved. He made everyone think for themselves.

Ohno once visited a factory and observed an operation. Immediately afterwards he told the assistant manager of the factory, "Get rid of that automatic delivery machine."

The assistant manager knew that his workers would be strongly opposed to the idea but followed the instruction without asking the reason why. Ohno was the Vice President of Toyota at the time and was responsible for the entire production line. His instructions had to be followed and no objections were allowed.

The assistant manager ordered his workers to carry out the instruction. Workers complained, as expected, saying,

> "If we remove the machine, how are we going
> to transport heavy items? We would need more
> workers and time. It would be extremely hard
> to perform the same job. Please tell Ohno that it

cannot be done."

The assistant manager thought it to be a reasonable reaction from his workers but he was unwilling to tell Ohno that. He told himself, "Mr.
Ohno must have a very good reason behind it.
I will follow his instructions for now and think
about a solution."

Ohno had instructed the assistant manager to come up
with a solution on his own. He did exactly that, searching
everywhere for a clue that would help him come up with
a solution.

Transportation by workers was out of the question. It
would increase the labor cost and become time-consuming, which Ohno would never agree with. He continued to
brainstorm for an alternative way to transport items without using an automated machine. He incorporated ideas
from his workers and decided to construct a special holding jig by which heavy items were lifted up and pushed
onto a destination. A pulley was also used to move items
while being lifted up.

In practice, it was much easier that they thought it to be.
It was a breakthrough idea and the task was performed
much faster than the automated machine. The assistant
manager fully realized what Ohno was after.

Ohno returned to the factory after a few weeks and did
not waste time in approaching the assistant manager.

"Is the shop floor doing alright without the automated machine?" Ohno asked.

"Yes, they are doing fine. Everybody brought
good ideas together. We decided not to rely on
increasing the number of workers, as it would
only lead to labor enforcement, resulting in a
higher overall production cost. We figured out
through trial and error that the best way was to
make use of a special jig and pulley. This new
method allows us to reduce the time required

for transportation as well," the assistant manager explained.

Ohno was quite content to hear this and replied, "That is wonderful news! Honestly speaking, I was worried for your workers after giving you such a difficult challenge. The shop floor workers bring out their hidden potential when they are pushed over the edge. I am so proud of you all."

The assistant manager was extremely happy to receive the compliment from Ohno and also felt rewarded by working so closely with his own workers. He would never forget the fact that Ohno had personally shown his concern and wished luck to the entire shop floor.

COME UP WITH THE ANSWER ON YOUR OWN

It is true that Ohno was known to give everybody the hardest challenges. As illustrated in the previous story, Ohno never gave out challenges for which he did not have substantial reasons or solutions of his own. It is possible to say that he had already known a solution to the problem that tormented the assistant manager. However, Ohno always refused to give away answers as he strongly believed in the innate intelligence of humans and the shop floor. It was this belief that had enabled Ohno to challenge the shop floor workers to go beyond the "possible" realm, even without giving out any clues.

Many managers today still do just the opposite. They may appear to be trusting the shop floor and believe in its potential but they end up giving out their own solutions to be followed. To this end, workers no longer apply their own intelligence to battling a problem.

Ohno used to say, "We can teach so many different principles to the shop floor workers, however true results can never be attained unless the shop floor workers begin to think on their own."

While management staff can think of many ideas, only the shop floor workers can come up with solutions that work because they are the ones doing the actual job. Ohno believed that the collective solution generated by the shop floor workers was the key to the entire process, which leads to success in the Toyota System. Ohno felt so relieved to see that the assistant manager was able to lead the shop floor to an effective solution, the shop floor would have experienced a disaster otherwise.

Ohno believed that the fundamental goal of continuous improvement was to make work easier for employees. Therefore it is the responsibly of the management to establish effective methods and provide help to their workers, so that their jobs can be simplified. The assistant manager had that deeply ingrained in him through his experience with Ohno. I am still amazed by how dedicated Ohno was to inspiring workers to draw their own answers. I am going to elaborate on that by using examples in the next chapter.

REASONING BEHIND THE TOYOTA SYSTEM

One can land on an incredible idea when pushed over the edge, however only pushing someone over the edge is not always a guarantee. It should be done by not only pushing workers through a hardship, but also by providing guidance whenever it is necessary. The goal is to inspire our workers so that they will find great joy in meeting our mutual expectations.

REVERSE YOUR THINKING PROCESS

STOP MOTHERING YOUR WORKERS

The motorization of society intensified around the year 1965. Toyota launched a project that sought a reduction in the total cost for updating a specific line of cars by 10 thousand dollars. It generally cost an average of 10 million dollars to do so at the time. The project manager, Mr.

G presented a plan to Ohno with a budget of less
million dollars. Mr. G was confident that his pla
be approved by Ohno since it was well under the average
cost and all other arrangements were already made. Ohno
glanced at the plan and said,

"This is one zero too many."

He did not say anything more, or give Mr. G any suggestions as to how to pull it off. Mr. G became completely
lost as to what to do. If it was one zero too many, he had
to create a plan under 1 million dollars. Ohno did not give
any clues to Mr. G. That was Ohno's way: to not give away
everything and make his workers think by themselves.

When I was involved in continuous improvement ac-
tivities, Ohno would often tell me to remove waste from a
certain process, but never told me how to do it. If I did not
have a solution even after serious brainstorming, I generally managed to receive some advice from Ohno, but nothing substantial that could lead to a solution. Ohno's way
was quite time-consuming and required a great deal of patience on the side of management. However, Ohno acted
on his belief that motivating workers to think on their own
was the best solution. Ohno used to scold a certain manger
who always spoon-fed his workers by giving out answers
too easily.

> "You are simply acting like a mom for your
> workers. That's the main reason why they take
> a long time to grow," Ohno said.

Reducing the cost from 10 million dollars to only 1 million dollars was an extremely challenging task, just as Mr.
G thought. He reflected back on what Ohno had taught
him in the past to draw a solution. Ohno used to say,

> "Continuous improvement is all about the fine
> balance between craftiness and money. Ad-
> vancement can be achieved by simply spend-
> ing more money, however continuous im-
> provement requires intelligence and craftiness.
> If too much money is spent on a project we will

cease to apply our craftiness to formulate a solution."

I cannot agree with this more. There are many ways to
make improvements in a process. The shop floor may decide to simply spend more money to yield an improvement, or focus on improving the process itself without
spending any money. If the latter can draw the same result
as the former it would simply mean a waste of money.
Therefore, it is advised that we first think of a solution that
does not require money.

Instead of saying, "Purchasing more machines can solve
the problem," we should ask ourselves, "How can we do
this without increasing machines?" This is how workers
can be inspired to devote their intelligence and craftiness
to a solution. With this in mind, Mr. G prepared a new
plan from scratch.

EXTREMELY DIFFICULT CHALLENGES CAN LEAD TO GROWTH

No matter how much Mr. G had been trained by Ohno,
it was not an easy task and the plan was put on a hold for
a while. However, Mr. G kept on thinking. It is human
nature to push out toward new ideas when we feel lost.
Mr. G continued to received some advice from Ohno and
finally reached a point where he thought his plan could
possibly work. His plan called for rearranging the shop
floor layout with the help of available workers.

The factory was completely remodeled and the production cost was significantly reduced, mainly by changing
the locations of conveyor belt production lines and running wires underground in conduits.

This achievement became a precious experience for every worker on the shop floor. Everyone learned the true
way of achieving continuous improvement; only by full
participation from the shop floor workers so that their
new ideas could be tested in practice, to draw the most
effective solutions. Everyone also appreciated Ohno, who
challenged them on their craftiness to make it happen un-

der such a limited budget.

Mr. H was a project leader in a Toyota-affiliated company that supplied Toyota Motors. He was considering building an additional facility to run his project in. Ohno happened to learn Mr. H's intention and told him,

> "Building a new facility brings a new array of fixed costs to your company."

The project faced a risk of being called off due to the high cost of building a new facility. However, Mr. H came up with a solution to launch the project without having to build a new facility for it. Ohno kept giving Mr. H new demands as the project progressed. Ohno kept saying,

> "The amount of equipment investment is too high."

> "Do not spend so much money on Automation."

> "Do not hire any more workers, to minimize the labor cost."

Ohno demanded nothing that was easy to achieve. Even for those as experienced as Mr. H was, giving up was always an easy way out. However, Mr. H chose to devote himself to achieving continuous improvement by applying the intelligence and craftiness of the shop floor. As he kept trying he began to witness gradual, yet steady, increases in productivity and profit.

It was everyone's commitment to meeting Ohno's hard-to-achieve demands that led to various successes of the company in continuous improvement, productivity, and competitiveness. Ohno's unique attitude towards work, and what he used to tell his workers, will always be remembered in an appreciative manner by those who had a chance to work closely with him.

REASONING BEHIND THE TOYOTA SYSTEM

Struggling to overcome a hard challenge by utilizing ones craftiness and suggesting new ideas eventually leads to an ability to think on your own. It is good to give yourself difficult challenges, such as limiting a budget, labor and production time. This will change the way you approach a problem and enhances your ability to implement the most effective continuous improvement solutions.

MOTIVATING PEOPLE REQUIRES SWAYING THEIR EMOTIONS, HOWEVER IT COMES WITH MANY DIFFICULTIES

SHOW YOUR COMMITMENT

Executive managers from an outside company once visited the Toyota factory. The company was not affiliated with Toyota in any way but was determined to implement the Toyota System into its production to survive tough market competition after the Oil Shock of the 1970's. At the time, Ohno was called the "god of the shop floor." Executive managers felt extremely honored by being guided by Ohno on his shop floor and being able to learn from him in person.

> During the tour Ohno stopped at a process line and started yelling at the production supervisor loudly. "I have told you so many times before but you never seem to understand. You are still creating waste because you have too many workers under you. Get rid of some workers! " he said.

Executive managers were shocked to witness the whole scene as Ohno turned into a completely different person. Ohno's yelling was echoing all over the factory and he was about ready to throw components at the supervisor. The reason for his anger was because the supervisor was instructing workers to overproduce. Even worse, the stock was excessively stored in a location where it was not supposed to be.

When it came to overproduction Ohno never allowed it, as he believed that overproduction was the biggest and most harmful waste. For this reason, he immediately ordered the supervisor to eliminate some of his workers. Even though Toyota had been implementing its stringent ways of production, and Ohno had devoted his career to teaching the adverse effects of overproduction, some production managers still lacked understanding and had a tendency to still rely on overproduction.

The tour participants learned that facilitating the principles of the Toyota System in every single worker was extremely challenging and required a great deal of passion and commitment to its implementation, as Ohno had clearly demonstrated. After the tour the company began overhauling their production system while continuing to receive instructions from Ohno, as well as other Toyota affiliates.

As the company was accustomed to a mass production system, it was extremely difficult for the company to shift towards the Toyota System. Even when the Toyota System enabled the production of 120 items they were only allowed to produce 80 items, given that only 80 items were demanded by the market. Then, they had to use their craftiness to lower the production cost as much as possible for those 80 items.

Additionally, the company had a strong labor union that criticized them, claiming that the Toyota System was causing unreasonable labor enforcement for its members. Executive managers emulated Ohno's commitment to the process and successfully overcame the resistance by persuading the labor union that the Toyota System was the only way to ensure the survival of their company.

STOP PRODUCTION AND GO PLAY INSTEAD

Company A was a supplier of Toyota and suffered from a low volume of sales and new business after the Oil Shock had broken out. They were also suffering from excessive inventories as the Toyota Production System was not fully implemented into their production mechanism. It was to a point where they might as well stop production altogether for a while and let the inventories run out completely.

The top management of Company A finally decided that they would become fully commit to the Toyota Production System and asked for Ohno's help. Ohno was glad to provide his assistance and said,

> "Follow the Kanbans that are given by Toyota. Make sure that your factory produces only the quantities that are instructed by the Kanbans from now on and stop producing unnecessary items."

> "If only the quantities indicated by Kanbans were to be produced, my workers would finish production by 2 or 3 o'clock in the afternoon and will be left with nothing to do for the rest of the day. I cannot lay off my workers so easily. What should I tell them to do with the spare time?" the management asked Ohno.

> Ohno simply replied, "Just stop production there and let your workers play around to kill time."

It would have been against the work ethic of full-time workers to just pass time on the shop floor, as they received salaries in exchange for putting enough hours in each day. Instead, the management decided to instruct workers to work on continuous improvement activities in their spare time. Each worker was given a lead on their own improvement ideas to achieve much bigger goals at the end. As a result, machinery maintenances and production line management began to see some improvements, which helped the company survive the tough times since the Oil Shock.

At first it was difficult for the shop floor workers to refrain from production when it was not needed. However, they were able to learn about the waste in overproduction by patiently carrying out continuous improvement activities, which also provided them with a feeling of reward for every positive result.

Harsh measures, such as the one in this story, were sometimes needed in order to establish the Toyota System firmly in place so that each worker on the shop floor felt like they owned every part of it.

REASONING BEHIND THE TOYOTA SYSTEM

It is common sense to say that only saleable items should be produced at all times. However, we often underestimate the challenge of doing so in practice. It is Toyota's way to give workers rough treatment and put them over the edge so that they will learn to overcome this challenge.

Hmmm—

Commandment 4

"Competitors are always smarter than you. The only way to win the battle is to start right now."

ACT ON PROBLEMS RIGHT AWAY, DON'T PROCRASTINATE

CARRY OUT CONTINUOUS IMPROVEMENT UPON IDENTIFYING PROBLEMS

In 1965, a Toyota-affiliated company introduced Automation in its production lines. Ohno visited the factory and asked the project manager, Mr. I, who was Ohno's subordinate,

> "Mr. I, come here. Why did you assign two workers to this automated production line? If it is malfunctioning just stop the line and call in the production leader or a technician to fix it. Explain to me why two workers were put to guard it from the beginning. "

It had been only a few days since Automation had been implemented in the production line and it was far from being perfect. For this reason, Mr. I decided to have two workers supervise it at all times. He knew very well that it was wasteful to do so but justified his decision because the machines were already misbehaving. He gave his apology to Ohno by saying,

> "These machines have been failing. I assigned two workers to supervise the production until the machines are fixed."

> "If the machines are not functioning, you must repair them right away. Have you even shown this to our technicians?" Ohno asked.

> "I have not done that. I have been too busy to do so. Besides, a repair of these machines is not so easy to accomplish," Mr. I said to convince Ohno.

> Ohno's face turned red with anger. "What do you mean you cannot repair the machines right away? Bring in the technical manager immediately! "

> "The technical manager is away in Tokyo on a business trip as we speak," Mr. I replied.

> "It does not matter where he is right now, just tell him to come back to the factory now!" Ohno pushed the envelope, as usual.

> Mr. I contacted the technical manager reluctantly and told Ohno that it would be after 8 o'clock in the evening when the technical manager could return to the factory.

> "Sounds good. I will wait here," Ohno simply replied and sat in a chair to wait for the technical manager.

Mr. I was astonished by Ohno's behavior. None of his superiors had ever called other managers away from their business trips to deal with a problem in the factory. They would, nevertheless, wait on the shop floor as Ohno so patiently did. However, this matter concerned not only Mr. I but also the whole company, as it was quite unusual for the Vice President to become so angry that he demanded managers to go out of their way to return to the factory. Mr. I nervously waited with Ohno without any idea what was going to happen once the technical manager returned.

The technical manager finally returned to the factory a little after 8 o'clock in the evening. Ohno simply said to the manager,

> "Thank you so much for coming back all this way. These machines stop unexpectedly. Can you take a look at them?"

He did not say anything more. Mr. I could not believe the change in his personality. Ohno had removed his angry look and was no longer intimidating to be around. Mr. I finally learned the purpose of Ohno's action. It was a lesson for him to learn to work harder and show more commitment to problem solving.

Mr. I had failed to follow a basic rule of Toyota, in which a production line must be stopped when there is a problem. The true cause of the problem, "Why do the machines stop in the first place?" was not analyzed and solved by continuous improvement methods. The problem was only patched by assigning two workers to supervise for the slightest possibility in which a malfunction could occur. That was what made Ohno blow steam out of his ears.

It was Ohno's belief that Automation needed to be equipped with a human intelligence that allowed automatic shutdown of the machinery if there was a problem. It could be done without the help of supervisors and the cost associated with maintaining them. Ohno used to say,

> "Distinguish tasks that can be done only by humans from those that can be done by ma-

chines. Do not use humans only as guards for
machines, instead assign them to the tasks that
can only be performed by humans. "

Mr. I was not following these rules at all and simply
gave up on fixing the cause of the problem right away.
Ohno again practiced a rough treatment on his workers
in this story in order to infuse the Toyota principles and
work ethics into the shop floor workers.

FIX THE PROBLEM IMMEDIATELY AND MOVE ON

No other person could match the rigorous attitudes
toward work than Ohno did. Ohno was simply one of a
kind. He never left a problem unsolved or unseen and did
not mind waiting for a solution for many hours. He would
tell a worker to fix something in the evening and expect
him to fix it by the next morning.

Many other managers often point out a problem to workers and leave it to them until it is solved. This does not motivate workers to fix the problem right away.

Ohno always made sure that his workers:

(1) Fixed the problem immediately after it was
identified.

(2) Confirmed the result with their own eyes.

What upset him the most was when problems were ignored and wastes remained in production as a result. Mr.
I was confident that he would not forget his experience
with Ohno. It has become his habit over the years to carry
out implementing continuous improvement immediately
after a problem is found.

REASONING BEHIND THE TOYOTA SYSTEM

The Toyota System finds it extremely important to initiate continuous improvement in actual practice and yield
an improvement within the same day as the problem is
identified. Apologies such as "It is getting late today" or

"I cannot get a hold of the supplier" are not only excuses but also the leading cause for increasing wastes in production.

DO IT NOW; YOU CAN SOLVE ANYTHING

YOU DO THIS ON THE WEEKEND? YOU MUST BE JOKING

Ohno visited a factory and questioned the improvement facilitator, Mr. J. "How is the worker's performance in that process? Is he ahead or behind the Takt-Time[1]?" he asked.

Mr. J had no idea and gave Ohno his honest answer. Ohno asked the same question to a section leader and was told that the worker was ahead of the Takt-Time.

"The section leader is obviously lying. I don't even have the answer. How could he have possibly known the answer?" Ohno told Mr. J.

Ohno took Mr. J to a meeting room and gave him instructions on the chalkboard. Ohno told Mr. J, "In your factory, it is impossible to tell who is doing their job well or not. That makes it challenging to assess the operation to find out what continuous improvement is needed. Show the starting point of production clearly by installing a pace maker in the line."

Mr. J consulted with production managers and reached a decision to install a buzzer. A week later Ohno returned to the factory and was told about the buzzer as a solution. Ohno looked at it and said, "You need to do something different. This kind of buzzer sound makes workers feel like they are always under pressure. Think of something more fun to listen to. Actually,

---

1 Takt-Time is the ability to match the rate of production to the rate of sales or consumption.

have your workers decide on which sound."

Ohno gave another order. "Place the buzzer in 3 locations instead of one location so that everyone can hear it better."

Mr. J listened to what Ohno had to say for the next 2 hours then Ohno asked a question out of the blue, "When do you think you can install the buzzer in 3 different locations?"

Mr. J went to ask the operation manager who said "We will do it over the weekend." He gave the same answer to Ohno. Ohno was not satisfied and told Mr. J a story.

"I visited a Toyota factory a few weeks ago. I saw a number of auto body frames hanging over the conveyor belts. I asked the department director to reduce that and he seemed to understand my instruction. I called on him after a couple of hours to see if he was successful in reducing them or not. He told me that he would deal with it over the weekend. So, I told him, 'I understand. How about I climb up there with a hammer and destroy every frame right now?' The director panicked and started working on it right away."

WHY ARE YOU STILL SITTING IN YOUR OFFICE?

Mr. J rushed into the shop floor immediately after he heard Ohno's story. It was as though Ohno asked Mr. J, "Why are you still sitting in this office?"

On that day, Ohno had to leave the factory at 4 o'clock. It was already 3 o'clock. Mr. J managed to have technicians relocate the buzzers with temporary wiring, by 5 o'clock. Mr. J went back to the meeting room wondering if Ohno had already left or not. Ohno was still sitting in a chair, even though he was supposed to have left the factory an hour earlier.

Mr. J learned later that Ohno had been sitting in silence since Mr. J left the meeting room. Other meeting participants had to sit around Ohno, who was not saying a word while waiting for any result to come in.

Mr. J told Ohno, "We finally did what you asked us to do."

Ohno immediately stood up from his chair and said, "I am leaving now."

"Please come see what we accomplished on the shop floor."

"No, I have to leave right now."

"Everyone worked so hard. The least you can do is to have a look at the improvement," Mr. J begged Ohno persistently and was told by him,

"You finally became motivated towards eliminating wastes. That's all I asked for."

Mr. J could never forget what Ohno had said to him and the whole experience has taught him the most important lesson of his career. Ohno hated nothing more than those workers who rely on others to solve apparent issues and have a tendency to procrastinate.

When a defect occurs, the production line must always be stopped to discover the true cause of a problem. Otherwise, wastes simply carry over and cause more serious adverse effects over time. Eliminating wastes upon identifying them is extremely difficult to achieve, though it is the most effective way.

REASONING BEHIND THE TOYOTA SYSTEM

It does not mean the end of your job after giving orders to different departments. You must make sure that your orders are carried out immediately. If your orders are being neglected, you must take the initiative just like Ohno did by climbing up the ladder with a hammer. Such vigorous behavior can effectively lead to motivating workers to take immediate action toward eliminating wastes.

YOU CAN FIND A BETTER SOLUTION TODAY THAN YOU CAN TOMORROW

BUILD UP A SOLID FOUNDATION

"My time has finally come."

In 1973, Ohno visited Tokyo with his wife to receive the Medal with a Blue Ribbon, given to individuals who have made prosperous efforts in the areas of public welfare and education.

> His wife said to Ohno, while looking at the stagnated downtown of Tokyo as a result of the Oil Shock, "It is sad to see downtown like this. The economy affected even the big cities such as Tokyo."

> Ohno replied, "The Toyota Production System is cut out for just such a time as this. During our high economic growth period in the past a profit was guaranteed no matter how we conducted manufacturing. But this recession has put an end to that. Only the truly effective production systems will help us survive from now on. That is why we have worked so hard to this point for the creation of the Toyota Production System. It is being put to the test now so that its true virtues will be revealed. "

I read this episode in another piece of literature about

Ohno, which reminded me of what Ohno used to say,

> "Rationalize production while enjoying a boom and build up the foundation work."

Ohno explained his ideas to me as follows.

> "In the automobile industry, truly positive results can be achieved only when a new model of the car is introduced while the existing model of the car is selling extremely well. It is true that some companies still choose not to introduce any updates while sales are going well with the existing models, however it is always too late to do so after the sales boom ends. Merely the introduction of new models cannot bring sales back on track. It must happen while enjoying a boom in sales.
>
> The same idea applies to the rationalization of production. It must happen while a company is experiencing a leeway in profit and time. If we missed that it would be extremely hard to improve production in the time of a financial struggle, which puts a hold on rationalization. In this case, some factories choose to eliminate their workers as a last resort, but this would be cutting away important muscle from production. Factories must focus on trimming excessive fat instead."

[handwritten margin note: Do Lean when times are good]

As Ohno explained the importance of rationalizing production while enjoying a boom he also put a great deal of his effort in spreading the Limited-Quantity Production System, which always promised a profit when either an increase or decrease occurred in production.

IF A PRINCIPLE IS JUSTIFIABLE, CARRY IT OUT

Ohno's principles were justifiable but were often turned down to be implemented into practice, especially when the economy was on a rise. In fact, the Toyota Production

System drew people's attention only after the Oil Shock. Before that most companies enjoyed the fact that more profit was surely expected, as more items were produced and maintaining inventories was an ideal way to keep up with the market demand.

Ohno's principle of producing only the saleable items, without stocking items, was never attractive to those factories. However, that was exactly what enabled Toyota to survive the Oil Shock period with more than sufficient profits.

> Ohno remembered those times and said, "There is nothing secret about it. I just got lucky that the sudden occurrence of the Oil Shock helped me prove the true virtues of my production system."

Ohno was being modest here. The Toyota Production System was already yielding positive results even prior to the Oil Shock. It was just that its true virtues remained unrecognized at that time.

> Ohno also said, "Our job is like building the foundation hidden under a building. True virtues of such a foundation are hard to understand as its physical appearance remains unseen by people. However, a building simply collapses without a strong foundation underneath it. Therefore, I have always conveyed the significance of achieving a rationalization of production and implementation of a strong I.E. (Industrial Engineering) as the foundation for manufacturing, despite the fact that they will remain unseen most of the time."

The strength of a foundation determines its endurance in a time of crisis. Ohno was not satisfied at all when the foundation survived through a crisis. Most companies are satisfied here. Instead, Ohno often fired up his workers to seek more continuous improvement in the existing foundation by saying.

"Do not leave our foundation vulnerable to a crisis. Fix the problems so that it will not suffer from a future crisis."

The origin of Toyota's sense of crisis goes back to what Kiichiro Toyoda said when he decided to resign from Toyota in exchange for receiving support from financial institutes in 1950.

> Kiichiro said, "In this era of economic instability, we will never know what is going to happen. Therefore, we must prepare ourselves on a daily basis so that we become able to eliminate our fear of facing a crisis and survive through various crises as a result. That is how a company begins to see its true potential and development, especially when a healthy economic environment finally comes around. "

With regards to being prepared for crises, Mr. Cho, the current president of Toyota, said the following about issues associated with human resources:

> "The main reason why a factory ends up with more workers than needed is that it is often overwhelmed by the amount of work to be completed. If a factory faces a different quota each day, it tends to overly assign human resources and equipment in order to accommodate busy days. However, if daily production is leveled, kind of like not creating any mountains or valleys, such excessive allocations would not be necessary.
>
> In terms of factories, busier factories also require more workers. This problem can be solved by transferring workers among different factories. The important thing here is that both processes and tools must be standardized so that workers are able to resume work without confusion and loss of time."

Toyota has accumulated even the smallest ideas and improvements over many years, with a great deal of dignity, by the hands of many great philosophers besides Ohno. This is why Toyota no longer fears crises and is always able to overcome difficult challenges.

REASONING BEHIND THE TOYOTA SYSTEM

The essence of voicing "Build up the foundation of work" comes from a strong commitment toward making jobs easier for workers on the shop floor. Preparation toward the future while solving each existing problem right away is the key. This will eventually establish a strong organic relationship of trust between management and the workers.

CONTINUOUS EFFORTS BUILD A SOLID FOUNDATION

DON'T UNDERESTIMATE THE SIMPLE TASKS

Mr. K was called onto the shop floor to learn about a certain problem. The problem would never have occurred if the worker had paid enough attention. After solving the problem, Mr. K visited Ohno and asked,

> "How come our workers fail to perform such simple tasks? Is it because our training was not enough? Or, are our workers completely incompetent? "

> Ohno's answer was quite surprising. He said, "It is considered a job well done if you can make sure that each worker completes his simplest tasks. In fact, everybody is having the hardest time in just overcoming that."

It is true to say that completing the simplest task repeatedly remains a real challenge. Ohno understands that clearly. That is why he used to tell workers to stop the production line immediately when a problem or defect occurs. After the production is stopped, workers should repeatedly ask themselves "Why?" so that the true cause of a problem can be revealed. Only asking workers to pay more attention at hand does not lead them to overcome the true cause. Rather, the same mistakes will most likely occur again in the future.

The Toyota System analyzes what causes carelessness in the first place and in doing so a real solution to the problem is discovered. On the other hand, most companies simply tell their workers to pay more attention. That is as far as they go because they think it is the minimum requirement for their workers to be careful at what they are doing. Ohno was aware of the difficulty in making workers do a minimum requirement all the time, that's why he challenged Mr. K to figure out how to possibly make sure that the workers do what they are supposed to do.

After this episode, Mr. K had begun to analyze and eliminate the true causes as to why his workers failed to perform their work, instead of simply yelling at them so that they would do their jobs right the next time.

Ishida Taizo once remarked about the challenge of following common sense in the most natural way,

> "Our way of management is in fact as simple and basic as it could be. However, the reality is that things do not always go as they are supposed to. Some managers choose to be creative and try to sell ideas that are out of the ordinary. However, my style is to consistently follow common sense in the most natural manner. In other words, I have always made sure that I did what had to be done. If something needs to be done, I devote myself to completing it while overcoming various other challenges. It is that simple."

THE TOYOTA SYSTEM IS BUILT UPON COMMON SENSE

Eiji Toyota once talked about how Toyota dealt with the Hanshin Earthquake of 1995. In his conversation, he also touched on the challenge of doing things by common sense.

As I mentioned repeatedly, Toyota factories make it a habit to stop their production lines every time irregularities occur. Such irregularities included natural hazards, such as the Hanshin Earthquake. Though Toyota did not stop production for any incidental reasons, such as shortages of components or workers failing to get to work due to the earthquake. Toyota proactively did so knowing that production must be stopped after any natural hazardous event of this magnitude.

Eiji said the following in regards to this common practice of Toyota,

> "Typhoons or car accidents can indeed stop components from coming into our factories. Toyota knows how to deal with that kind of situation and trains their workers accordingly in advance. That's why Toyota remains flexible when it comes to stopping production."

In other words, Toyota considers it common sense to stop when problems occur. Eiji also knew the challenge of ensuring that. He said,

> "The Toyota System does not have secret weapons or anything like that. We are just following common sense and we make sure of that. Even that alone is extremely hard to implement in a large organization like ours."

It is quite reassuring to learn that Ohno, Taizo and Eiji shared the same principles. "Do not produce defects" and "Produce only saleable items" are the most basic and fundamental common sense rules that the Toyota System is built upon. However, no other companies have ever been as capable of adapting the Toyota System as well as Toyota itself did. This is because they lack the commitment to practice common sense thoroughly. The difference between those who understand the importance of analyzing solutions and those who do not can be used to explain their failure. The challenge of enforcing common sense must be acknowledged as it is the only way to lead us to solutions.

REASONING BEHIND THE TOYOTA SYSTEM

It is a challenge to enforce common sense or practices onto your workers. Have you ever been frustrated with yourself or your workers when a simple task failed? You may have asked yourself, "How is it even possible for a common practice to fall behind?" There is no better time than that for you to ask yourself your definition of common sense.

Commandment 5

*"Remove any limitations in your work. Don't just do
what you are told to do, use your craftiness to go one
step further."*

DON'T FEEL SATISFIED BY SAYING, "I FINISHED THE JOB" GO BEYOND THAT AND SAY, "I CAN DO MORE"

THOSE WHO ONLY FOLLOW MY INSTRUCTIONS ARE FOOLS

Ohno visited a factory where a young Toyota worker, Mr. L, was working on continuous improvement along with his colleagues. Ohno observed their activities carefully for a while and approached Mr. L, when he was taking a small break.

> "Do something about that process after you finish what you are doing now," Ohno told Mr. L and left the shop floor without disclosing what needed to be improved in the process. Mr. L and his team were completely lost as to what to do.

75

Ohno came back to the shop floor in the early evening and asked Mr. L, "Have you done anything to fix the process?"

"We have not done anything because we do not know what is wrong," Mr. L gave Ohno his honest answer.

This time Ohno described the problem to him, as if to say, "Why can't you find out just by looking at it?" Mr. L stood on the shop floor the next day collecting ideas to fix the problem.

Ohno approached him and asked, "You have fixed the problem by now, right?"

"No. I went home last night thinking that I would start today," Mr. L replied.

"I see. When you put it off for one day, it means that you are making everyone else suffer for one more day. I don't understand why you did not start immediately," Ohno said.

Mr. L did not waste any more time and started formulating a continuous improvement strategy, though he struggled to gather up his ideas and failed to yield any results all day long. Ohno came back to the shop floor again asked to see if there was any progress.

Mr. L said, "We are brainstorming to find a solution, but our ideas are just not good enough yet."

Ohno gave Mr. L some useful hints and told him that he would come back to see the results the following morning. Mr. L knew that it had to be done today, however he still could not generate any better ideas and time was running out. He simply completed what he was instructed to do by Ohno hoping that it would be sufficient. As promised, Ohno came back to the shop floor early in the morning and asked the same question. Mr. L replied with confidence and explained what he had done to improve the process.

"Yes. We fixed the problem yesterday," Mr. L said to Ohno.

Ohno replied with anger, "Why did you do only what I had told you to do?"

It was a harsh remark from Ohno. When Ohno asked the shop floor workers to fix something in the morning, he would come back to see a result in the evening. If he asked in the evening, he would come back the following morning.

Continuous improvement takes time, especially when new ideas have to be brainstormed to draw effective solutions. This time-consuming process often left no choice for the workers but to complete Ohno's orders in time. However, no matter how well the workers met Ohno's instructions, they were always scolded for having done only what they were told to do.

In many other factories they would have been complimented for the job well done but this is not the case with Toyota. The Toyota System requires something extra from workers. Workers must contribute their unique craftiness to achieve something beyond what they are ordered to do.

DO NOT BECOME A "CATALOG ENGINEER"

A Toyota worker, Mr. M belonged to the production management department of the factory. A problem occurred in the factory one day, which caused a significant delay in a certain process. The production management department was responsible for bringing the process back up to speed.

Unfortunately, Mr. M's supervisor was not present to provide any assistance, so Mr. M had to take a leadership role in solving the problem. Mr. M remembered that the same type of a problem had occurred in the past and decided to repeat his supervisor's solution to overcome the problem at hand.

His supervisor finally returned to the factory, but did he make a complimentary remark on how Mr. M dealt with the problem? The answer is no. He scolded Mr. M instead, saying,

> "The problem you encountered this time may have been similar to the one I had dealt with in the past, however they are fundamentally different from one another. Why didn't you try to come up with a more effective solution of your own?"

It is exactly like what Ohno used to say, "Only fools do what I tell them to do." I have had similar experiences myself and have seen many other colleagues in the same boat. Toyota believes that real work requires intelligence and has to be acted upon with commitment and responsibility by the workers. Ohno would refer to those whose performance was based solely upon what they had learned from reading manuals as a "Catalog Engineer." You would not be able to expect anything creative or innovative from those workers.

> Ohno criticized such workers behavior by telling them, "A competition cannot be won unless you incorporate your own unique craftiness into a strategy as much as possible."

If a manual tells us to use three workers to perform a certain task, we must find a way to do the job with one or two workers by continuous improvement. This can be achieved by implementing a mechanism in which production stops itself automatically when problems occur. Ohno called this mechanism "Automation with Human Touch" and encouraged giving human intelligence to machines in order to limit labor.

REASONING BEHIND THE TOYOTA SYSTEM

The Toyota System believes that the probability of winning competitions depends on how much human intelligence is incorporated into a strategy. Do not just read a book and do as it says. Do it better than that by utilizing your own craftiness. That is the Toyota way.

DON'T JUST FOLLOW INSTRUCTIONS, ADD YOUR OWN CRAFTINESS TO IT

IF THEY DO IT WITH 3 PEOPLE, WE WILL DO IT WITH ONE

In 1955, remarkable and innovative high-tech machinery was develop in the United States and was taken advantage of by General Motors and Ford to boost their productivity. Nissan had more financial resources than Toyota at that time and decided to implement the machinery into their production as well.

Toyota was known to be careful about investing in new equipment but decided to purchase the machinery, as a last resort to reduce their production cost, and did so by borrowing some money. The technician in charge asked Ohno to come visit the shop floor so that he could inspect the new machine.

> Ohno asked the technician, "Did you invent this machine?"
>
> "No, it was developed in the US," the technician replied.
>
> "Only Toyota has this machine in Japan?" Ohno asked.
>
> "No. In fact, Nissan started using it long before we purchased it," the technician answered.
>
> "So, we paid a lot of money for shipping to get this machine here. Say we produce our cars using this machine and export them to the United

States market. It means that American auto makers are able to produce their cars for much less cost, and even then we still have to pay shipping to get our vehicles to the US. How do you expect us to make a profit at all? And why did we assign 3 workers to operate this machine?" Ohno asked the technician.

"That's how they do it in the US," the technician replied.

"I have no idea how Nissan does it. If Americans require 3 workers we will find a solution so that only one worker can be responsible for operating the machine. Or, would you be happy with less pay if we choose to do it like the Americans? Do it with only one worker by all means, use everybody's craftiness to make it happen. That is the only way we can win the competition, and your pay will increase as a result," Ohno said.

Ohno's reasoning is as follows. Toyota purchased the same machine at a much higher cost than American companies because of the shipping and insurance expenses. Toyota still sought to make profits by shipping their cars back to the US. If Toyota still wanted to sell their cars at reasonable prices like their American competitors, the only way to do this was to keep the labor cost extremely low.

Ohno never approved of anything like this. In order for Japanese companies and workers to become competitive on a global scale Japan had to incorporate their unique intelligence and craftiness into their techniques. Ohno thought it was the only way that Toyota could survive. As a matter of fact, the technician who had been scolded by Ohno generated ideas and managed to assign only one person to the job in a few months.

ALWAYS DO MORE

Toyota has come to appreciate their great financial resources. Toyota has also gained the capability to develop their own machinery, incorporating robotics technologies with the help of affiliated vendors. However, because of the fact that Toyota became financially challenged in 1955, they had to rely on machinery that was imported from the United States for a long time. Toyota was determined to earn profits in foreign currency on the market, which was dominated by the much stronger General Motors and Ford. Therefore, Ohno was strongly against the idea of operating the same machinery in the same way as Americans did in order to make their dream come true.

Additionally, if we look at the global market, there are a wide range of goods and services that are inexpensive. Such inexpensive goods and services must not be ignored in order to keep the production cost competitively low. Some companies are wrong to believe that inexpensive goods and services fail to maintain a good quality. Inexpensive prices can be explained by the fact that such goods and services are often produced in countries where a labor cost remains extremely low. However, the Toyota way is to produce even better items in Japan, despite a labor cost that is relatively high, so that they can fully oversee the quality of their products.

REASONING BEHIND THE TOYOTA SYSTEM

If you simply move your factories to other countries only to save labor costs, you will end up repeating the same process once the labor cost starts going up in the country you moved to. Toyota does not depend on relocation to reduce their labor cost. Instead, they find their own way to do so internally by generating new ideas and strategies.

AVOID A UNIFORM TREATMENT OF SUPPLIERS, IT ONLY LEADS TO LABOR ENFORCEMENT

USEFUL TOOLS CAN TURN INTO DEADLY WEAPONS

Useful tools can cause adverse effects if misused. One of the techniques invented by Ohno, the Kanban System, is a great example of that. There was a time when it caused a serious misunderstanding among companies because it was implemented in a wrong manner.

In early 1975, the relationship between the auto industry and component suppliers became awkward because of the wrong application of the Kanban System. The reason was a dramatic increase in both the volume and types of components, due to the motorization of society. It was also a time when people were big on individuality and purchased one-of-a-kind items, which required factories to conduct low volume production of a wide variety of products. However, many factories continued to carry out mass production to accommodate the market demand, which led suppliers into having to maintain stocks to supply factories with the necessary components in time.

Auto industries should have reviewed their own production style to mitigate the supplier's risk of holding inventories. However, they chose to implement a Kanban System in order to reduce their own inventories and not supplier's. Kanbans instructed suppliers to deliver only the necessary items in the necessary quantity at the right time. Suppliers became panic-stricken by this demand.

It was quite understandable for suppliers to react that way. Suppliers had been accustomed to mass producing items and were aware that the only way to accomplish the demand from auto makers was to maintain inventories. They also knew the negative effects of doing exactly that. The Kanban System was designed only for the benefit of auto makers and was often referred to as "Supplier Bullying." This issue was even discussed in the Japanese Parliament, where the Kanban System was suggested to be terminated. Since then Toyota, being the creator of the

Kanban System, has come under public scrutiny.

REAL KANBAN AND FAKE KANBAN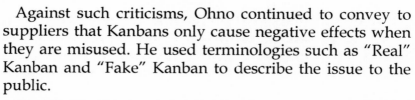

Against such criticisms, Ohno continued to convey to suppliers that Kanbans only cause negative effects when they are misused. He used terminologies such as "Real" Kanban and "Fake" Kanban to describe the issue to the public.

The Kanban System is based strictly upon "Just-In-Time" and is not only a method of ordering items. Production in a parent company must be leveled in order to make the Kanban System successful. In other words, the Kanban System becomes effective only after the production of a parent company becomes optimized by conducting continuous improvement.

That is what Ohno always did first on the shop floor when adapting the Kanban System in a new environment. It was only after this process that the Toyota System was introduced to suppliers and the Kanban System could be adapted with effective results. As long as this rule is followed, the Kanban System is able to reduce inventories for suppliers and also give suppliers necessary support for internal reform. That is a "Real" Kanban System. On the other hand, a "Fake" Kanban System, also referred to as "Supplier Bullying," can be described as follows:

A parent company forces a Kanban System onto its suppliers for their own benefit of not having to hold inventories in its own factories. It also pushes a selfish ordering process to suppliers, which increases the volume of their inventories. For these reasons, a "Fake" Kanban System does not yield anything positive and can completely destroy suppliers.

Ohno devoted himself to implementing only a "Real" Kanban System with suppliers. The success of Japanese manufacturing industries, as well as global industries, contributed to his commitment, which had overcome a significant level of criticism against the Kanban System in the past. As a person who has witnessed Ohno's tremendous effort, I personally give my gratitude and respect to him for this accomplishment.

When the level of criticism was still high against the Kanban System, a Toyota worker, Mr. N, was assigned to work under Ohno to reform the entire production system of a food processing company. In the beginning, Mr. N intended to implement a Kanban System but rejected this idea after discovering that production had not yet been leveled to accommodate a Kanban System.

The biggest number of orders were being received on Sundays. If leveling was to be forced into production, it could mean that an excessive amount of inventories had to be maintained and their company goal of "Delivering Fresh Items to Consumers All the Time" would be impossible to achieve.

Mr. N's solution was to forget about incorporating Kanbans in production and reformat the production line based on another Toyota principle, the "Pull Production System." This Build-to-Order production system allowed the factory to gain a constant flow of profits, even fluctuating sales by establishing flexible manpower lines. One day Ohno visited Mr. N on the shop floor and was told,

> "We decided not to use Kanbans, but we are getting positive results with the 'Pull Production System.'"

> Ohno complimented him by saying, "Kanbans are only a tool. As long as you are after the same goal, it does not matter at all if you are using the 'Pull Production System.'"

REASONING BEHIND THE TOYOTA SYSTEM

An unfamiliar method or technique can turn into a deadly weapon. You can prevent this from happening by internalizing it and making it your own. Apply your intelligence and craftiness to a solution, do not just follow manuals.

DON'T TEACH YOUR WORKERS EVERYTHING, LET THEM REALIZE ON THEIR OWN

DON'T MAKE ARRANGEMENTS FOR EVERYTHING

A Toyota worker, Mr. O, received instructions from Ohno to lead continuous improvement activities in an affiliated factory. The company was receiving a growing number of orders from Toyota and needed to expand production by adding supplemental production lines. Management did not want to rely on the help of a third-party specialist and decided to do it on their own by asking Ohno for assistance. Ohno sent Mr. O to help.

Mr. O had been involved in many continuous improvement projects before but this was the first time that he was fully in charge. Mr. O was committed to devoting all of his knowledge and experiences to establishing new production lines and achieved serious progress over time. At first the factory was skeptical of Mr. O but they learned to trust him, as he had been assigned by Ohno. When they agreed on the final strategy plan for expansion, Ohno visited the shop floor and asked,

"How is the expansion going?"

Mr. O explained to Ohno every detail of the plan he came up with. Ohno listened to him for a while then replied harshly,

"You came up with every idea and are about to carry it out under your supervision. You must be proud of yourself. But, you're not leaving any room for the factory workers to get involved in the planning processes. Your job is not to come up with solutions for them. Your job is to put them on the right path so that they can solve their own problems with their knowledge and experiences. Don't get it confused."

Mr. O admitted the fact that he had been pushing his ideas upon the workers instead of listening to their ideas.

It is not to say that his ideas were useless, Ohno simply did not want to see him becoming an "eat-your-peas" figure and ignore the demand of the shop floor workers to be able to find their own solutions.

Applying intelligence to work must be promoted by inspiring workers to incorporate their intelligence into their own work. For example, what happens when a consultant gives a company only standardized work sheets to follow in the process of adapting the Toyota System for the first time? It may make it look like the Toyota System but it is far from being a true implementation.

A Toyota worker once presented his thoughts on the definition of "effective continuous improvement,"

> "Effective continuous improvement cannot be achieved without a cooperative effort from the shop floor workers. We (management staff or advisors) may think that our ideas can earn a perfect score, but we always end up scoring only 50 points out of 100 when they are put into practice on the shop floor. Only the shop worker can tell us what really needs to be done and how it needs to be done. That's the only way that our solutions can get us closer to a perfect score."

If one becomes a management figure, he tends to enjoy his authority to tell people what to do. Some managers mistake continuous improvement activities to be an opportunity for them to make initiatives. Such managers must learn that bringing out innovative ideas and knowledge from the shop floor workers is the role of managers in leading continuous improvement. Or rather, a manager should be a helper and not an instructor. That's what I learned from Ohno.

FOLLOW A STEP BY STEP PROCESS IN ACHIEVING CONTINUOUS IMPROVEMENT

Mr. O reviewed the entire continuous improvement process from the beginning. Even thought it became more time-consuming, he formulated a set of new solutions by borrowing knowledge and ideas from the shop floor workers. As a result, the whole continuous improvement process ran more smoothly in practice because worker's ideas were reflected in the solutions this time. Mr. O visited the factory a few months later and was astonished to see much greater improvement than he had expected. At the same time, he discovered what Ohno had meant by "Production Line with Human Intelligence."

For several years after Mr. O left Toyota, he continued to work as a consultant helping companies implement and adapt the Toyota System to their needs. He always kept in mind that continuous improvement must be achieved on a step-by-step basis. He had encountered factory managers who demanded a substantial change and improvement to occur based only on his ideas as quickly as possible due to a lack of time. Mr. O always advised against such managers by saying, "We must take time in the process and allow your workers to generate their own ideas so that their accomplishment becomes much more meaningful to all of us."

REASONING BEHIND THE TOYOTA SYSTEM

Create an environment where your subordinates are always encouraged to formulate their own solutions through a trial and error process. Take time and guide them through the process one step at a time. If you make all the arrangements for them, they will simply do what they are told and stop participating in the problem-solving processes and this is how your company loses its competitive edge.

Commandment 6

"Avoid demanding obedience and respect your workers by giving them a long-term view."

ADD "APPROPRIATE TIMING" TO "APPROPRIATE METHOD" IN PROBLEM-SOLVING

BECOME A DEPENDABLE LEADER

A young Toyota worker, Mr. P, was working on continuous improvement on the shop floor. A female worker came to the shop floor and told Mr. P, "The factory manager wants to see you immediately." The factory manager was Ohno and every worker was intimidated by him because of his explosiveness. Mr. P put his work aside and ran towards Ohno's office, wondering what he had possibly done wrong. When he arrived in Ohno's office he was out of breath and white-knuckled.

Ohno told Mr. P, "It took no time for you to come to my office on such short notice. It is evident that you're not needed on the shop floor. In fact, if you were in the middle of important work and are depended upon by your workers, you would not be able to leave the shop floor right away, as you just did. You should have told the female worker that you were too busy and you would come here after you were done. If the matter was so important to me, I would have visited you on the shop floor anyway."

Mr. P was angered by Ohno. It was a common sense to report to superiors immediately after workers were buzzed. Workers could not simply tell their superiors that they were simply too busy to follow instructions.

Of course, Ohno knew that Mr. P would come running to his office like everyone else. Despite this, Ohno called him in to teach him an important lesson. I have had similar experiences as Mr. P. Ohno used to give this reasoning behind his action,

> "A leader in continuous improvement activities must be deemed dependable and trustworthy by his workers. He must proactively initiate continuous improvement as he sees it in order to make worker's operations easier. This will win their respect and generate an expectation toward future improvements.

> "Every time you visit the shop floor, workers ask their leader for more advice for improving the shop floor processes and environment. In this way, a leader probably needs several hours just to walk 100 meters. On the other hand, if a leader fails to initiate continuous improvement, workers lose respect over time and simply ignore the leader. Walking 100 meters would be a piece of cake."

DON'T BRAG ABOUT YOUR AUTHORITY

Ohno's lesson "Become a dependable leader" left a strong impact on Mr. P's career. After this encounter with Ohno, Mr. P had many opportunities to lead continuous improvement solutions in many companies outside of Toyota. He made it a rule not to brag about his authority as a Toyota affiliate and established close communication with the shop floor workers on a daily basis.

In the beginning, workers were suspicious of Mr. P's overly friendly manner. But they started to trust him, over time, to a point where they would ask his advice for even the most serious and personal of problems. He jumped on fixing such problems right away. When a worker asked for his help in the evening, he would stay after work and find a solution so that the worker need not suffer from the problem another day. Workers began to depend on him more and more for his advice, which was easily accepted, on a daily basis.

The biggest payback came when he was placed in charge of the large-scale production reform of a factory. Despite the fact it was a challenging reform, workers followed his instructions without a doubt based on the strong relationship they had built over time.

Mr. P later performed the President role of many companies. He always stood by his rules and was able to salvage unsolved continuous improvement strategies into successes, just like he learned from Ohno.

Ohno was not the type of person who bragged about his authority, or one who refused to cooperate with the shop floor workers. The next section describes this attitude in detail.

REASONING BEHIND THE TOYOTA SYSTEM

A close relationship with the shop floor workers is necessary in order to draw their ideas and craftiness into problem-solving. This is done by becoming a dependable and trustworthy leader. A dependable leader always draws dependable workers to work under him. The Toyota System defines a true leader as someone who pays respect to his subordinates instead of forcing prostration by his authority.

GIVE YOUR WORKERS CARE AND TIME SO THAT THEY START APPROACHING YOU

I AM PATIENT

While Ohno worked toward implementing the Toyota System in Toyota itself, he proactively introduced the principle to the suppliers that conducted business with Toyota. Today, the Toyota System is considered to be the standard, and a minimum requirement for manufacturing to be successful. However, it was usually up to companies that had a strong desire to adapt it in the past. Ohno never minded spending much of his time in teaching these companies, as long as they were fully committed and good listeners.

In 1965 a component supplier for Toyota decided to implement the Toyota System in its production. Mr. Q, from the production department, was put in charge of the implementation. He was told by the president that the future of the company was depending on his effort and gained a strong commitment to achieving successful results. He visited Ohno several times and attempted to carry out every instruction. However, no matter how hard he tried, he was not able to convince either the shop floor or any other departments to offer their cooperation in the process.

> He asked the president, "Could you give me more authority so that the opposing departments will follow my instructions? It will make the whole process run much more smoothly."
>
> The president replied, "I understand the reason why you're asking for more authority, but why don't you discuss this with Ohno first?"

He visited Ohno and explained the situation to him.

Ohno asked, "Are you available only today? Are you also available tomorrow?"

Mr. Q answered, "I am available as long as it takes to find a solution."

Ohno replied, "Okay. Let's go see one of my factories right now."

Despite the fact that Ohno was an extremely busy person, he went out of his way to guide Mr. Q through a series of Toyota and Toyota-affiliated factories. Ohno did not intend to explain anything in particular to Mr. Q on the tour.

Having spent 2 whole days touring almost every factory in the neighborhood, Ohno finally asked Mr. Q, "Have you figured out what you were trying to solve yet?"

Mr. Q replied, "Yes, I definitely did. I learned so much by observing the shop floors with my own eyes."

Ohno asked again, "Have you noticed anything unusual?"

Mr. Q gave Ohno his honest observation.

"I did witness some inappropriate application of the Toyota System in some factories. I was wondering why you did not instruct the workers to correct it as we walked through."

Ohno answered, "I am being patient. I cannot use my authority to force them to do what I want them to do. It would not lead to good-quality products. What we must do is to persistently seek understanding from the shop floor workers by persuading them of the true virtues

> of the Toyota System. After all, manufacturing
> is essentially a human development that de-
> pends heavily on how we teach our workers."

At the time, Ohno was the Vice President of Toyota and was in charge of the entire production process. In spite of his status and authority, he insisted that work must not be led by those who are only of higher status and authority. Mr. Q appreciated Ohno's leadership tremendously and felt honored by having been able to learn this important lesson in person.

> "He (Ohno) must have been too busy to teach
> a young and non-Toyota-affiliated worker like
> me, but he spent two whole days so that I could
> learn," stated Mr. Q. He was so appreciative of
> Ohno that every time he remembered the expe-
> rience it brought tears to his eyes.

CONTINUOUS IMPROVEMENT IS A STEP-BY-STEP PROCESS

We need to remember that a certain level of authority and leadership is needed in the implementation of the Toyota System. However, that is not everything. It is often quicker to bring changes and yield immediate results when management simply tells workers what to do. In this way, there are many cases where everything reverts back to the original state when a management or surrounding environment changes. Ohno took advantage of his status and authority to a certain degree. However, he concentrated on encouraging his workers to actively identify problems and engage in continuous improvement.

I was extremely impressed by his attitude. No matter how much time it required, Ohno always made sure to embed the ability of continuous improvement into his employees, who later became continuous improvement promoters on the shop floor and did not experience any drawbacks.

Nurturing workers and creating a climate for continuous improvement ideas were Ohno's principles. Ohno demonstrated these principles to Mr. Q by the method of "Visualization" on the shop floor. Ohno taught him the importance of patiently persuading workers of the benefits instead of simply giving orders.

After Mr. Q returned to his own company, he began to ask himself repeatedly some fundamental questions such as "Why is the production reform necessary in the first place?" and "What are the true virtues of the Toyota System?" When he ran into problems while conducting continuous improvement he made sure to involve every shop floor worker in the process of formulating effective solutions to overcome the challenges, one by one. Eventually, the shop floor was filled with workers who always said to each other "Let's carry out continuous improvement!" and Mr. Q accomplished his goal of reforming production with great results.

REASONING BEHIND THE TOYOTA SYSTEM

Workers will devote 100% of themselves to performing work in which they see value. On the other hand, they fail to yield positive results from work in which they do not see any value. Workers may also show resistance to change, especially when ordered to alter the way they always performed their work. Instead of telling them to simply follow orders from a superior, explain thoroughly to them why such a change is necessary and patiently persuade them to see the true benefits of such a change. This is the essence of motivating and nurturing your workers.

SHOW WORKERS WHAT YOU CAN DO FIRST

SEE, IT'S NOT THAT HARD

Anxiety associated with replacing an old method with a new method is much larger than we can imagine. Especially with the Toyota System, which demands a leap in the way of thinking and performing work that can lead to ambivalence and resistance among workers. It is a management leader's responsibility to effectively draw ideas from such workers, in the process of a reform.

To persuade workers that showed resistance to change, Ohno focused on demonstrating his ideas on his own. He conducted experiments to show workers the real results of his principles in practice. Consultants or management can tend to overwhelm workers with theories from text books, but workers fail to see their applicability to real practices on the shop floor and show rejection. Consultants are somewhat important, but Ohno conveyed the importance of leaders who could carry out principles and show the actual results to workers. Ohno always said,

> "The most important thing in the Toyota System is to have trainers who can carry out their own instructions themselves and persuade workers by showing how much they alone can accomplish. If a trainer demonstrates for only a couple of hours, workers may still reject it for the reason that they have to do it from 8:00 in the morning until to 5:00 in the evening. In this case, a trainer should perform for the entire day. This kind of persistence will persuade the workers and motive them to accept new changes. Let them want to accept the changes. That's the secret here."

The Toyota System is *not* labor enforcement. It is just that Toyota's innovative methods can double or triple production, which leads workers to believe that they have to work harder. However, this is simply an illusion. We must explain to workers that it is a result of elimination of waste and rigorous continuous improvement activities that causes the increase in productivity. We must also make sure that workers are motivated to take part in continuous improvement by seeking their understanding of the true purpose and demonstrating principles in practice, as if to say "Look how effective this is. Even I can do it. So, can you!"

ADVANTAGES OF A "MODEL LINE"

The use of a "Model Line" can bring greater results than simply aspiring to try continuous improvement. For example, a supplier is asked to reduce their inventory down to one-week of supplies, instead of one-month. The shop floor thought it was impossible and showed their resistance to the idea. In this case, Ohno would single out a particular production line to be altered, instead of changing production entirely.

A small-lot production system was necessary in order to reduce the amount of inventory. Changeover time for machinery also had to be reduced from one hour to three minutes. A single production line was altered so that these challenges were met and workers received hints for continuous improvement to make things more effective. Through these experiences workers were able to observe immediate results and began to appreciate what the Toyota System had to offer.

When Ohno visited factories in China for training, he used the same method to train their workers. He picked one production line and operated it under the Toyota System. As a result, it required only one person to complete a certain process, which required six to eight workers prior to continuous improvement. The factory manager saw this dramatic improvement and demonstrated that he too could perform the job by himself. "The factory manager is doing the job all by himself. There is no way we could not do the same," the floor workers observed and gained their reassurance toward the principles of the Toyota System.

REASONING BEHIND THE TOYOTA SYSTEM

The true purpose of a principle must be observed in practice instead of simply understanding its logic. Top executives and managers must do more than just be guides. They must demonstrate their ideas and principles to workers so that they can visualize the results. This is the most effective way to motivate their workers, not by their status or authority.

DON'T LET WORKERS SWEAT OR THEY WILL LACK IDEAS

THERE IS NO NEED TO GIVE ADVICE

A Toyota worker, Mr. R, worked in the administration department in the early part of his career and was later appointed by Ohno to lead continuous improvement activities in the production department. At the time the shop floor was far from designing and developing information systems (I.E.), which imposed a large challenge upon Mr. R to yield positive results.

> Ohno supported him by saying, "It is not as difficult as you think to improve the shop floor. All you have to do is apply common sense where it is needed."

The shop floor workers would tell Mr. R that administrative staff not only lacked useful ideas but also were unwilling to spend money for improvement. They also thought it was wasteful in and of itself for someone as inexperienced as Mr. R to try to identify wastes on the shop floor. Mr. R did not know if he should have felt angry or encouraged by these remarks.

> "Don't worry about what people think, just do your best. You cannot make the shop floor any worse than it already is," Ohno would tell him whenever he was unsure about working on an improvement.

As he continued to receive Ohno's encouragement, he gradually acquired positive results from his continuous improvement ideas. In the beginning, he would make sure to get Ohno's advice before he did anything. However, Ohno would never give him detailed instructions or answers for his problems, he would only give advice when his ideas were outside the bounds of the Toyota System and put Mr. R on the right path. It was not much help, but Mr. R appreciated it from bottom of his heart.

One day, as Mr. R was on his way to Ohno hoping to receive his advice as usual, he came to the decision to carry through his own ideas without Ohno's advice this time. He retraced his steps back toward the shop floor and carried out his own continuous improvement ideas. It turned out that he was able to achieve the result he had hoped for. Since then, he received Ohno's advice much less frequently.

> Mr. R told me once that, "Ohno's advice helped me establish a good foundation and provided discipline to my solutions and actions. Because of that, I had come to the point that I could carry out my ideas and be confident about the results without any help from others."

THE IMPORTANCE OF A COLLECTIVE THINKING PROCESS

As I mentioned in the previous chapters, Ohno never gave out answers to his subordinates. Ohno's way was mentioning two out of ten ideas, and his subordinates had to think of the rest themselves. There are many managers these days that turn over the entire thinking process to their subordinates and refuse to participate in problem-solving processes. These managers do nothing but criticize their subordinate's ideas in the end. This is not the way it should be. As Ohno used to say,

> "Work is essentially a battle of ideas between managers and their subordinates. When you lead a large group of workers, it is true that you have to act strictly toward them, however your leadership is not strictly giving orders. It should be founded on the collective thinking process with your subordinates. When you give out orders, consider them as orders given to you at he same time, and then solve problems with your workers."

The "Battle of Ideas" requires managers to think to the point where they are able to give effective advice to their subordinates while still keeping their own answers to themselves. Ohno also said,

> "If you cannot give advice to your subordinates
> when they are completely lost, you should have
> never given out your orders in the first place."

This was basically Ohno's stance toward the collective thinking process. Eiji Toyoda made similar remarks for mangers in various departments. He said,

> "I want everyone to use your brain. It is trou-
> blesome to have your subordinates do all the
> thinking for you. I am not asking you to deal
> with all the trivial issues. However, you all
> must train yourselves so that you will learn to
> generate your own ideas for the most critical
> issues."

Mr. S, a subordinate of Ohno-trained Mr. R, shared the following experience with me. He received an extremely difficult test to solve from Mr. R and could not find an effective solution to overcome it, no matter how hard he tried. His colleagues agreed on the difficulty of the challenge but could not help him out. He approached Mr. R and told him honestly the clear reason why he could not pull it off. He was given one more day to think about it, but the result was the same and he reminded Mr. R once again of the reason why he failed this time too.

> Mr. R simply told him, "Okay, I will assign
> somebody else to this problem."

He did not mean to be rude, but it was quite insulting to Mr. S, who would have preferred to be kicked in the back and ordered to pull it off no matter what.

> The next day Mr. R called on a depressed Mr.
> S. "Don't feel so down. Let us put our heads
> together to tackle your problem. It is possible
> to solve it," he told him encouragingly.

The lesson to be learned here is that neither giving reasons nor excuses will ever lead us to a solution, but collective thinking and cooperation can achieve just that.

Eventually, Mr. S was able to find a solution to the problem with the help and useful advice received from Mr. R.

REASONING BEHIND THE TOYOTA SYSTEM

Supervisors have a responsibility to help their subordinates become astute thinkers. If a supervisor relies upon his subordinates to do all the thinking and fails to give useful advice, he disqualifies himself to be in a leadership role in the realm of the Toyota System.

Commandment 7

"Say "I can" first. That's how you find a solution."

BELIEVE IN "I CAN" AND QUESTION "I CAN'T"

YOU MUST AT LEAST GIVE IT A TRY

Ohno used to talk about how he had learned from so many masters when he established the foundation for the Toyota Production System. Ohno learned from such principals as:

- **"Automation"** by Sakichi Toyoda
- **"Just in Time"** by Kiichiro Toyoda
- **"Flow Production"** by Ford Motor Company
- **"Scientific Management System"** by Frederick Taylor

The most famous episode of his is that he came up with the idea of the Kanban System from a supermarket. After

World War II ended, Ohno participated in the implementation of various production systems, such as Multi-Process Handling. However, he had a hard time eliminating a basic assumption in the manufacturing industry that production had to flow from earlier processes to later processes. This assumption disabled him from helping factories reduce the volume of inventories by a significant margin. To solve his problems he analyzed the mechanism of supermarkets in the United States. Through his research, he was able to attain a breakthrough idea that allowed earlier processes to produce only the quantity indicated by later processes. He also invented the mechanism of the Kanban System in order to operate "Pull Production Systems."

I strongly believe that it was Ohno's diligence in repeatedly asking himself "Why?" that enabled him to find the solution to this challenge. I imagine it was like Newton discovering gravity by a falling apple.

What was most amazing about Ohno was that he always took decisive action to carry out his ideas on the shop floor. Of course, reversing assumptions is a hard thing to do. However, reversing conventional practices is even more challenging to accomplish. That is exactly what Ohno did. Someone once said to Ohno,

> "I've read a lot of books but I always fail to apply what I learned to the shop floor."

> Ohno replied, "What you learn from reading books is not usually useful when it comes to improving the shop floor. You will find much better ideas by just trying different methods on the shop floor."

> Ohno also said the following in terms of "giving it a try" on the shop floor:

> "I too have had a hard time in convincing workers to carry out my ideas. Humans essentially do not like to be told what to do. But, humans are prone to be influenced by proven princi-

ples. There was a time when our competitors were better than Toyota and had proven the effectiveness of their ideas. I used to persuade my workers by telling them how our competitors achieved their successful results. That's how I would get them to try anything in the first place."

DO NOT FEAR FAILURES

When Ohno took on the responsibility of implementing the Toyota System, he did not have much authority over anything. All he had was his strong commitment and dedication to achieving great results. Labor Unions often demanded that top management put a stop to what Ohno was trying to reform. However, the top management, including Ishida Taizo, Eiji Toyoda and Syouichi Saito, were always supportive of Ohno and allowed him to continue his endeavor. Ohno appreciated their understanding from the bottom of his heart. When Mr. Saito passed away, he showed his sincere appreciation of him to everyone, with tears in his eyes.

"I am who I am now because of Saito, along with many other great masters," he said.

He also presented his deep gratitude toward Eiji by saying,

"If the outcome of my action was obvious, it would be so much easier for anyone to lead me in the right direction. But, obviously nobody knew what my clear intentions were. In spite of that, Eiji placed a great deal of trust in me. That's why I was free to use my ideas; so that I could achieve the results I really wanted. "

Eiji Toyoda described the time when Kiichiro Toyoda was attempting to implement his idea of "Just-In-Time" in the newly-constructed Koromo Factory.

"Waste-free production systems may have been impossible to realize, but we must start working toward our ideals instead of just arguing if it is possible or not. It is important to believe in yourself and take initiatives with your confidence, " he stated.

Ohno inherited these work ethics and applied them toward his goals. Toyota has always cherished the mentality of "Just give it a try first" because of the founder of the Toyota Group, Sakichi Toyoda. Of course, Ohno was the same way and would not put up with people who simply gave up and presented their excuses without even trying. As I mentioned earlier, I cannot ever forget how Ohno used to say to such people "When did you become a fortune teller?" Ohno may have appeared to be a short-tempered leader to say something like that, but he always had personal warmth in saying, "Do not fear failures and just give it a try first."

Ohno once said to a manager who was criticizing a mistake made by a young Toyota worker,

"You are being too strict toward your workers. That's not good at all. If your workers are motivated enough, they decide to give it a shot even without promising results. In such cases, it is very important not to make them feel guilty for failing. Otherwise, they will begin to fear their mistakes and lose their passion for trying new ideas. You can be a strict leader as long as you provide them with a helping hand."

REASONING BEHIND THE TOYOTA SYSTEM

In rare cases, continuous improvement can unexpectedly lead to an adverse effect. However, this is not a justification for putting everything back to the original state. If you criticize mistakes too much, workers will fear mistakes and stop trying their ideas in the first place. Instead, encourage them to repeat continuous improvement over and over, so that unwanted results can be eliminated and something positive will eventually come out of it.

EVERYBODY HAS INNATE INTELLIGENCE; IT IS THE ROLE OF LEADERS TO EDUCE SUCH INTELLIGENCE

DIFFERENCE BETWEEN IDEAS AND KNOWLEDGE

Several Toyota workers and retirees were sharing a meal one day. An active Toyota manager described his concerns to the retirees by saying,

> "Everyone is trying so hard and working over-time every single day, but we never seem to have enough time nor labor to accomplish our goals."

> A retiree said to the manager, "You're lacking one more thing. Do you know what it is?"

> The manager replied, "I have no idea. What is it?"

> "You're lacking good ideas. That's the reason why you're always complaining about the lack of time and labor. Try to generate more ideas and get them to work from now on," he replied.

That is something Ohno would say for sure. He always used to say,

> "Toyota employs so many people, however very few people have good ideas. We must nurture more people who can generate good ideas."

Ideas are different from knowledge. Anyone can acquire knowledge by reading books or attending school. In other words, knowledge can be readily purchased. On the other hand, ideas are acquired by ones own experience. Your ability to generate ideas can be enhanced by a series of thinking processes you practice on the shop floor. That is to say that your ideas are tied strongly with your actual achievement.

Some manager once made Ohno extremely furious for saying to him "I cannot do it" before he had even tried it. Ohno did not like such an attitude to begin with, though he had another reason to be mad this time.

> "There are many workers under your super-vision. You're underestimating the potential of your workers. They can surprise you with ideas when they become serious about it. How dare you give up instead of inspiring workers to generate their unique ideas!" he said to the manager.

Ohno used to tell managers to intentionally give work-ers a hard time so that they would find themselves in an environment where their ideas were absolutely necessary. This manager not only did not believe in his workers, but also failed to show any desire to nurture his workers. As a result, he failed to teach them the most important prin-ciple, "Give it a try first."

HOW DARE YOU SAY YOU CANNOT DO IT?

It is because of the fact that many dedicated workers gen-erated and practiced their unique ideas religiously on the shop floor that Toyota has been able to sustain continuous improvement for more than 50 years. Toyota's "Original-ity Movement" initially began around the process of gen-erating individual continuous improvement ideas. As the quality control activities became poplar, it developed into a "Collective Idea" movement. This is when the quality of continuous improvement suggestions became extremely high among Toyota workers.

What is the merit of collective idea generation? If you think alone, you tend to think of something that is unreal-istic and irrelevant to the real issue. Say you are overtired from your daily work, there is no way you can come up with good ideas. Ohno was aware of this phenomena and came up with a strategy. He put group leaders in charge of collecting small ideas from each worker and formulated a large-scale continuous improvement solution based on such "trivial" ideas. Ohno explained this as follows:

> "For example, 10 people are thinking about a continuous improvement idea. Let's say each person comes up with an idea. The group leader consolidates those ideas and turns them into one big strategy in the most practical manner to guarantee a positive result. Such a strategy formulated in this manner is the most effective and relevant to the real challenge we face. It's like the saying 'Many drops make a flood,' so make sure you pay attention to every little idea."

Ohno adhered tenaciously to his belief that,

> "Humans are extraordinary beings, and there is no limit to human intelligence. Each person was born with a certain degree of intelligence. Our responsibility is to inspire people to use their intelligence to generate new ideas. That's why I always put them on the spot."

REASONING BEHIND THE TOYOTA SYSTEM

It is true to say that simply giving up without trying at all abandons your ability to generate your own unique ideas. At Toyota workers often say "I am going to generate ideas" instead of "I am going to work." They find their work extremely rewarding when their own ideas become the reason for successful results.

DON'T BELIEVE WHAT CRITICS SAY AND DON'T BASE YOUR JUDGMENTS ON CRITICISM

WHY DON'T YOU GO DO IT YOURSELF?

A subordinate of Ohno, Mr. T was assigned the full responsibility of planning and designing the floor layout of a new factory. The factory started its operation without any difficulties but suffered from a low volume of orders due to the economic slump at the time. However, it is the Toyota way to always find a way to generate profit, even in a down time. Mr. T managed to survive the situation by focusing on increasing the efficiency of workers and machinery by various continuous improvement methods.

When the recession was finally over and business started to pick up for the factory, it was ordered to increase production drastically. It was a hard challenge for the factory to shift towards much greater production as it had prepared itself for production in a minimalist way. Mr. T repeated continuous improvement and enabled the factory to produce items in much larger quantities. However, he could not bring the casting process department up to speed. Mr. T was troubled about this and visited Ohno for his help.

> He told Ohno, "Our casting process is failing to keep up with the production quota, therefore our production cannot be increased any more."

> To this Ohno replied, "Why don't you go and work in the casting process to help them out."

Mr. T was very confused by what Ohno told him. At the time, the casting process was oblivious to the Toyota System and conducted mass production that was led by skill-oriented and somewhat selfish workers. Mr. T had no previous experiences in a casting process either. How would he possibly be able to help them out?

Mr. T stepped into the casting process and learned that

the situation was worse than he had expected and the shop floor workers were reluctant to follow his orders. What was worse was that Ohno kept coming back to the shop floor and scolding Mr. T for not making any progress.

Mr. T worked overtime on a daily basis convincing the workers to carry out his continuous improvement ideas. He would come in to work before anybody else, improving the production line so that it could start the casting operating immediately without any loss of time. He kept telling himself, "I need to try everything on my own."

Positive results of continuous improvement can never be achieved by simply using your authority to give orders. It would only achieve temporary results and workers tend to lose their focus without constant supervision. The shop floor workers are not motivated enough for their job, in such a case.

Mr. T listened well to what each worker had to say and incorporated their ideas in his solutions. By doing so, he was able to gain understanding and cooperation from the workers and, despite the fact that it took more time than expected, he finally accomplished his goal of bringing the casting process up to speed.

THE FAILURE OF OTHERS IS NOT YOUR EXCUSE

There are many reasons why things do not go the way they are supposed to. You or your department may be the reason. At the same time, other people or departments could be the reason as well. As for the latter, if you tell your supervisor, "My process is doing well but another process is falling behind. That is the reason why we cannot achieve our goal," the supervisor often agrees that there is nothing that can be done about it. However, Ohno was not like that. Ohno had his own theory, "Those who choose not to go beyond their responsibility and easily give up their effort in solving problems are merely imposing their own responsibility onto others."

If a problem occurred in factories or companies other than my own, I was often told to find a solution as if the issue was my own. Manufacturing must essentially have a flow through many processes on a large scale. It means that not only your company but also your affiliates have to be problem-free and maintain healthy relationships at all times. When there is a problem elsewhere you have to go there and fix it yourself. That is the Ohno way.

A construction company finally brought itself to adopt the Toyota System in production, as they outsourced most of their construction work to other companies at the time. As the amount of public works contracts decreased the company agreed that the only way to survive the competition was to reform its entire construction system in order to provide their services, in the way of "better and less expensive services in a faster cycle." They created a list of standardized work processes with help from their outsourced construction companies and repeated various continuous improvement strategies while sampling certain parts of their operation.

At the same time, they worked with suppliers directly to attempt shifting toward "Just-In-Time." In doing so, outsourced companies that understood the purpose showed their cooperation. Some companies failed to provide any help, even though they understood the purpose. Those companies seriously lacked the ability to generate ideas for achieving continuous improvement.

Workers who were in charge of promoting continuous improvement in successful companies were dispatched to unsuccessful companies and were instructed to yield positive results as if the problems were their own. Some dispatched workers succeeded in establishing effective standardized work processes and spent as long as two years making sure that continuous improvement was carried out to guarantee their result. Through these methods, this construction company became an organization that could yield substantial profits and dividends regardless of business conditions.

REASONING BEHIND THE TOYOTA SYSTEM

If there is a problem, go to the actual place and solve it yourself instead of just criticizing it as if it does not concern you at all. This is one of the most fundamental practices that we can do to facilitate the ability to get things done.

IF YOU WANT TO IMPROVE HOW WORK IS PERFORMED YOU NEED TO REFORM THE BASIC MECHANISM OF WORK

WORKING HARD DOES NOT ALWAYS MEAN DOING REAL WORK

Leaders who feel that their workers are doing enough work by simply observing them running around in a sweat will fail to accomplish any continuous improvement. It is a big mistake for leaders to highly evaluate workers only for their working overtime or even on weekends. I do not mean to say that such workers are not dedicated to their work, however leaders need to pay more attention to *how* their work is being completed. Toyota believes that "opportunity for continuous improvement is lost without a leader's attention to details."

Ohno once visited a factory for inspection and paused himself at the engine-assembly line. Ohno observed the shop floor workers for a while and asked the group leader,

> "Why are they lifting up the main engine compartment by hand?"

> The group leader replied, "Our vertical roller conveyor is being repaired. Until then, we need to manually lift them up. "

> Ohno asked again, "When did it break down? When will the repair be done?"

The team leader could not give Ohno a definite answer.

That implied that he was not even sure if he had processed a repair request for the machine or not. Ohno became infuriated about this and told the team leader,

> "What is the point of making them lift up such heavy items one by one? They are simply wasting their energy and getting nothing done. It is your responsibility to eliminate such waste and formulate effective alternatives to make their job easy in a situation like this."

> Ohno always told the shop floor managers, "Your job is not to teach your workers anything. Your responsibility is to simply help them out and find a way to make their work simpler, even for a bit."

Every time Ohno saw the shop floor workers running around in a sweat to manage their tasks, he would find their supervisors and scold them by saying, "The reason why your workers have to be running around like that is because your strategies and directions are so poor."

OBTAINING RESULTS EFFORTLESSLY IS THE BEST WAY

Ohno's fundamental goal in continuous improvement aimed for simplifying the tasks of the shop floor workers at all times. This is to say, workers can refrain from performing meaningless tasks by eliminating wastes and will begin to conduct truly productive work with enough time to spare. The key is that the shop floor managers and continuous improvement promoters must sympathize and eliminate a workers circumstances of hardship and tiredness on the shop floor so that they will be able to perform their jobs calmly and methodically.

Supervisors also need to be aware that a worker running around in a sweat does not necessarily mean that he is doing productive work. Execution of an idea is important, but there is a big difference between that and just running around.

There was a time when a certain Toyota factory experienced only half of its regular production load due to weakened productivity. In spite of that, when Ohno visited the factory, he discovered that every worker was working as hard as they had been.

> "Why is everyone running around like that when there's nothing to do?" Ohno asked a worker.
>
> "We get bad reviews from our supervisors if we're not doing anything. So, we are doing some cleaning and getting ready for tomorrows work, " he replied.
>
> Ohno called in the supervisor and scolded him severely. "If workers have nothing to do, the best thing to do is just have fun while doing nothing. It's simply a waste of money to have them work overtime just for the sake of it."

Ohno used to humorously say "JIT the workers." JIT (Just-In-Time) also means "to stay put" in Japanese. Japanese tend to worry if they do nothing in their working hours and feel compelled to do something unnecessary. They may run when there is no need to, or take on a difficult job on purpose in order to give a good impression of themselves to their supervisors when in fact they should strive to always keep a cool face and achieve definite results. This is how work should be done and is one of the most important goals in continuous improvement.

When we visit factories that are experiencing a financial crisis due to a low productivity rate, we often find workers that are overworked, even on weekends. Despite their efforts, factories fail to achieve their goals and the quality of their products remains noncompetitive. It can be said that there is something seriously faulty in the way they conduct their work. Workers are just wasting their time doing meaningless tasks and only appearing to be busy. Ohno always criticized this and taught supervisors an important lesson.

REASONING BEHIND THE TOYOTA SYSTEM

When you supervise workers or perform certain tasks as a worker, you must ask yourself important questions such as "What is the purpose of the task?", "Why do we move in the way we do?" and "Why do we perform tasks in a certain predetermined way?" Answers to these questions are extremely valuable when we seek continuous improvement. The Toyota System removes various types of wastes and helps their workers accomplish positive results effortlessly. This is Toyota's "Yes, I can" mentality.

Commandment 8

*"Learn from mistakes so that you can acquire true
confidence in yourself and increase the likelihood for
success in the recovery process."*

THE KEY TO ACHIEVING PROGRESS IS TO NEVER GIVE UP

A CRISIS EQUALS AN OPPORTUNITY TO GENERATE NEW IDEAS

Humans—as well as corporations—are put to the test
in the face of a crisis. Since a bankruptcy crisis of
1950, Toyota has faced many other critical moments such
as:

> (1) The Automobile Free Trade Agreement This
> is when Toyota felt threatened by the United
> States big three manufacturers (General Mo-
> tors, Chrysler, and Ford.)

> (2) The second Oil Shock

(3) Japanese Muskie Act[2]

(4) Strong Yen

(5) Globalization

(6) Environmental Issues

These crises could have easily pushed Toyota over the edge if appropriate measures had not been implemented. In fact, they did not become serious problems, as the financial crisis of 1950 did, for Toyota. It was because Toyota has always been capable of overcoming serious challenges since then because Toyota views crises as new opportunities and maintained a positive attitude.

Ohno, especially, always seemed to have been eagerly waiting for a crisis or problem, as he perceived it to be an opportunity to take a significant leap toward progress. Therefore, he would always encourage his workers, including me, not to fear crises or mistakes any longer.

When the first Oil Shock broke out, the production manager asked Ohno for his help.

> "We're facing a lack of components and an increased number of orders due to the Oil Shock. What am I supposed to do in a situation like this?" he asked.

> Ohno replied with encouragement, "Nobody knows the answer to your question, but you should consider yourself extremely fortunate to run into a problem like this while you're still in charge of managing production. This is the greatest opportunity to prove yourself and overcome challenges with your own ideas."

Ohno seriously thought that workers could engage in satisfying work in an event of unprecedented crisis, that was not limited to the Oil Shock.

---

2 *Also known as the Clean Air Act Extension, from 1970.*

Ohno said the following in a different situation,

> "As far as I'm concerned, it is more rewarding to be assigned to work in a struggling sales department than a successful department, as there is more demand for innovative ideas to continuously improve the situation. However, the reality is apparently the opposite. It's troubling to hear that most people assume that working in a successful department is more satisfying and miss a great opportunity as a result."

As far as Ohno is concerned, crises bring us the opportunity to generate new ideas resulting in greater continuous improvement and a competitive edge over others who do not.

WHEN THE TRUE VALUE OF A HUMAN CAN BE REVEALED

I believe that Ohno's way of thinking originated from the time of the Korean War, when he had to try everything in order to meet growing demand with limited production resources of labor and machinery. Around the time of Korean War:

(1) 1,000 trucks were produced per month by only 7,000 employees.

(2) 2,000 workers were forcibly released due to a labor conflict.

(3) On top of these pre-existing conditions, Toyota received an order of 15,000 trucks per month to be supplied for the Korean War.

Nobody had a solution to produce 15,000 trucks by only 5,000 workers. They barely managed to produce 1,000 trucks with 7,000 workers in the past. Ohno had no choice but to ask his workers to work overtime; however, the workers demanded of Ohno to bring back the fired workers. Since Toyota managed to avoid the risk of bankruptcy, Toyota could not afford to hire any more workers. Ohno was also under strict orders from the president of Toyota at the time, Ishida Taizo, not to increase labor in any situations. In addition, the Supreme Commander for the Allied Powers imposed extremely diligent quality standards on Toyota, no exceptions. It was indeed a tough time for Toyota. Ohno said the following while discussing his reminiscences,

> "I knew that we couldn't meet the production goal by our conventional production method and the order from my superior had to be carried out no matter what. I spent many days brainstorming for a solution and couldn't sleep some nights just thinking about it."

There was neither enough money, people, nor machinery. It is true to say that Ohno's desperate effort for formulating effective solutions triggered the birth of the Toyota Production System.

> Ohno also used to say, "The true value of a human being can be determined in a case of unprecedented crisis, where he can either decide to keep trying all the way or simply give up."

REASONING BEHIND THE TOYOTA SYSTEM

It is important to view problems and challenges as an opportunity. Of course, it requires a great deal of commitment to overcome such difficulties. However, unexpected results and skills can be acquired through the process of desperately seeking an answer.

Don't Give Up Because It's Destined To Become A Failure, Generate Ideas So That It Won't Fail

TOO MUCH LEEWAY IS NOT A GOOD THING

It is extremely embarrassing for vendors to produce defects or cause delays in delivery, therefore vendors put a great deal of effort into their production processes to avoid these errors. However, Ohno also instructed us to reduce the amount of Work-In-Progress items and finished product inventory, as well as the number of workers. He would say the following in regard to this,

> "If delivery delays are avoided this time, delay it the next time. If defects are eliminated this time, allow some defects the next time."

This is completely the opposite what Ohno had preached all the time. What did he mean by that?

After a long interval, Ohno visited the company that had implemented the Toyota System under his supervision. Ohno's instructions enabled the company to have relative success in production with the help of the Toyota System. The production manager reported to Ohno with a great deal of confidence, saying,

> "There is a slight delay in production on a daily basis. However, it has had no negative influences over our monthly production output. Thanks to all of your help, everything has been operating really well for us here."

> The production manager was hoping to please Ohno. However, Ohno gave him a hard time instead by saying, "You haven't experienced any real delays in production yet? You have not fought with your back to the wall! I urge you to do some real work here."

Ohno had good reason to say something like this. If Work-In-Progress items and inventories were reduced to the lowest amount possible and workers had to operate with limited resources, problems such as defects and delays would be inevitable consequences and it would not matter if every effort was made to prevent them from occurring. In other words, if there is too much leeway in production to begin with, this prevents the existing problems from surfacing and hides opportunities for continuous improvement away from us. It is extremely important to reduce the amount of Work-In-Progress items and the number of workers so that the real problems can be identified and appropriate continuous improvement strategies can be applied to the production process.

> "You have such a spoiled way of thinking. Execute your duties with a sense of urgency," Ohno would say to reprimand workers for their carelessness.

Other companies were also given the same instructions by Ohno when implementing the Toyota System under his supervision. When an excess amount of Work-In-Progress items are maintained, a production delay can be easily accommodated without stopping the production line. Prior to Ohno's instructions, the company was accustomed to operating under mass production systems in which they made it a rule to maintain a large number of Work-In-Progress items.

As instructed by Ohno, the company managed to reduce the amount of Work-In-Progress items to 3 items. However, Ohno was not yet satisfied and ordered them to reduce it down to one item. After repeated continuous improvement, the goal was achieved while experiencing a decline in the rate of operation. Ohno gave another order to reduce it to zero this time. His reasons are as follows,

> "Zero Work-In-Progress items is the ideal. We must acknowledge the true purpose of reducing them, though. We are not competing for who has the least number of Work-In-Progress items. If we have too much of it, we will fail to identify problems, that's why we must strive to reduce it.

"Reduction of Work-In Progress items causes the production line to stop. This does not mean that the reduction was the cause, it means that there was a serious problem with the shop floor to begin with and that the problem has been hidden due to the abundant amount of Work-In-Progress items. If we start seeing a problem as a result of reducing such items we must fix it immediately by continuous improvement. Repeating such an effort will enable us to reduce it to zero."

THE TOYOTA SYSTEM PROMOTES THE VISUALIZATION OF PROBLEMS

Some people state that adopting the Toyota System leads to more problems, but this is a fundamentally wrong assumption. A production system that operates under abundant amounts of labor and inventories is less likely to experience any defects or delays. On the other hand, if such resources are reduced by the Toyota System the strength of production will be brought to the surface. If it is strong enough, defects and delays will be more apparent problems. The Toyota System is not to be blamed for this. Everyone should know that the real problems are being covered up by our maintaining excessive labor and inventories.

The Toyota System enables people to visualize critical problems. We must take on the challenge of depriving ourselves of more-than-sufficient resources so that we will begin to identify problems and initiate continuous improvement measures to solve them. For example, with the absence of Work-In-Progress items a production line must be stopped immediately when a problem occurs. This is exactly when workers equip themselves with a strong determination to eliminate identifiable problems by continuous improvement.

"Neither excessive delays nor defects are ever acceptable, but a certain amount of defects or delay can be present at first so that workers can learn to visualize problems. If there are no delays or defects it means that you have too much allowance in production. You must purposely eliminate the amount of Work-In-Progress items and limit available labor in order to place workers in challenging situations. That's how problems can be exposed and passion for continuous improvement is derived within workers."

Ohno told this repeatedly to his workers. He strongly believed that real work requires us to maintain a sense of urgency at all times and being in a desperate situation can be the only way to make substantial progress, in some cases.

REASONING BEHIND THE TOYOTA SYSTEM

Some companies often say to their management staff "Cut down the labor" or "Reduce inventories." They are simply misunderstanding that the true objectives are simply to eliminate or reduce the production costs. Moreover, if a shop floor lacks the ability to conduct continuous improvement successfully, such a strategy leads to some adverse effects or chaos on the shop floor. There was a time in which a company got the idea of laying off a number of workers from reading some books on the Toyota System. Immediately after that, the company ended up receiving a large order, which brought panic to the shop floor.

We must remember that the goal is to bring problems to the foreground and make sure that effective solutions are applied to eliminate such problems. We must also pay attention so that our demands for reducing labor and inventories, as well as putting workers in a desperate situation, do not lead us to any form of labor enforcement by mistake.

IF YOU WANT TO GAIN STRONG SUPPORT FROM YOUR WORKERS, GIVE OUT FEWER ORDERS

THE TRUE PURPOSE IS NOT TO BE TAUGHT

A Toyota worker, Mr. U, had gone through rigorous training with Ohno. When he was an assistant production manager he made a big mistake on the shop floor. Mr. U was in charge of processing body frames for Toyota's Crown[3] series and designed an innovative production line for it.

Although Mr. U is still proud of his overall accomplishment, he regrets the serious mistake he made while using the "Power and Free Conveyors" system that he designed. The same mistake could have been easily avoided by an experienced worker, but Mr. U was not even aware of the fact that he was doing something wrong to cause the problem. What kind of a mistake was it? I do not want to be too technical here, so I am going to describe the situation simply for you.

The Power and Free Conveyors operates with a number of trolleys that run continuously on a chain to transport items. When a certain number of items are to be transported, a sufficient amount of trolleys must be present in the buffer zone. Mr. U failed to make sure of just that. He tried to transport 15 items while there were only 5 trolleys in the buffer, which caused the entire conveyor system to get stuck and the chain to break. Mr. U did not realize it was his fault and attempted to repair the chain instead. Ohno saw the whole thing and discovered the true cause of the problem.

> Ohno yelled to Mr. U, "It's not your job to fix the chain. Call the vendor!"

> Mr. U said that had no idea what exactly went wrong. Ohno became even more furious and asked, "What the heck do you think you're doing? Is this your first time working with the

---

3 *A high end model in Japan.*

Power and Free Conveyors?"

Mr. U, answered, "Yes sir, it's my first time operating this machine."

Ohno was upset with Mr. U when he saw the problem, but calmed down upon learning that it was his first time operating the machinery.

Even though it was after working hours for them, Ohno drove Mr. U to the Kamigo Factory in his own car. There was nobody working in that factory, since it was a Saturday, so Ohno turned the lights on and started demonstrating various processes to Mr. U. He continued doing so without uttering a word. He finally said to Mr. U, after one and a half hours, "Okay, that's enough."

Ohno drove Mr. U back to the head factory and told him to go home. That was it. No explanations were given to Mr. U the whole time, even when they were on the road.

Mr. U had the hardest time figuring out what went wrong. He did manage to learn, however, that there was something faulty with his Power and Free Conveyors and was determined to fix the problem immediately in order to resume production. He knew that there was a solution in the Kamigo Factory but was not completely sure what, as Ohno had not told him what the true meaning of the trip was.

WAITING PATIENTLY FOR AN ANSWER

Average superiors would have simply yelled at workers when they made such serious mistakes and assigned more experienced workers to the job, so that the same mistakes would not reoccur. They may immediately give out detailed instructions on how to fix problems. Ohno never did either. He simply showed Mr. U the Kamigo factory, that was it. Ohno simply said to Mr. U,

"This is how the Power and Free Conveyor is supposed to operate. Observe how I do it and compare that to how you were operating it.

Then, find your own answer to solve the problem."

It was a while before Mr. U discovered what he had done wrong in terms of retaining trolley buffers. He wished to immediately fix the problem, however, the production line could not be stopped any time soon and he had to wait until their summer vacation to take any actions about it. Ohno understood the situation and did not bother Mr. U any more, until the summer vacation came along. Mr. U finally fixed the problem by continuous improvement in August, as he had planned, and told Ohno about the good news when he returned from his vacation. Ohno simply said, "I see" and nothing more.

Ohno always had a short fuse and demanded his workers fix problems immediately after they were exposed. On the other hand, he trained himself to be extremely patient toward nurturing his workers. It would be the simplest and easiest solution if someone with the answers gave out his guidance to everybody so that problems could be solved right away without any confusion. However, Ohno did not like this way at all.

I remember that some of my colleagues were also helping out their subordinates by giving out answers, which deprived them of the opportunity to generate their own effective solutions. Ohno used to describe these people as being like a mother who was being overprotective of her children. "Formulate your own unique solution" was one of the most significant doctrines of Ohno for everyone.

Ohno was exactly the same way in the case of Mr. U, who had made a serious mistake. No matter how time-consuming it could be, Ohno was extremely patient in bringing his workers back on the right track of the Toyota System by providing them with useful suggestions and hints so that they could lead themselves to the right solutions. Scolding workers by saying "Why are you doing what I told you to do?" was therefore an effective method for Ohno to promote his way of teaching.

REASONING BEHIND THE TOYOTA SYSTEM

It may be quicker and easier for managers, or a company as a whole, to take care of any problems by providing workers with answers. It provides the assurance of problem-solving and is less stressful for both sides of the equation. However, this method does not allow workers to fully establish their own thinking ability. Your patience and commitment toward nourishing workers is put to the test when real problems are in need of effective solutions. There is simply no better time to do so than that.

SEE THROUGH THE NUMBERS; ONLY THE SHOP FLOOR CAN VALIDATE THE TRUTH

REASONS WHY LIES EXIST

Company reputations can be badly tarnished by scandals that often involve the manipulation of critical data. Such data is often submitted to pass governmental requirements or quality inspections, which in turn leads to a severe public distrust toward such companies in the long run. To a certain extent, any results or documents are generally influenced by the opinions and interpretation of their producers to begin with and the true fact of the matter becomes hidden as a result. One of Ohno's trainees once introduced his unique episode of "liars are bad people, however those who believe in lies are fools" as follows,

> "If you base your judgments on documents you received, you're most likely going to make wrong decisions. If you have even the slightest doubt in the information you received, you must step onto the shop floor for verification. For example, there was a president of a company who did not have sufficient technical knowledge, as he had been accustomed to mainly administrative types of work. Therefore, he made it a rule to visit the shop floor

whenever he faced uncertainty with the documents given while an executive meeting took place. Consequently, he often discovered that what had been told in the meetings were false assumptions.

This also created an impact on those around the president. Executives learned the fact that the president frequently visited the shop floor, which made them refrain from giving inaccurate information to the president any longer. It may be exaggerating a bit too much to say that around half of third-party information consists of lies. However, if management staff did not fully comprehend the shop floor, or lack the interests in analyzing the real problems, it would be inevitable that a certain degree of their lies and biases would be fabricated into their reports."

In another example, some spectacular reports are often presented in front of presidents and executives, as if they were true, in meetings to discuss positive continuous improvement results. However, such reports sometimes turned out to be completely false after visiting the shop floor. Information and scientific data were manipulated to publish desirable reports, in this case, to seek acknowledgement from the top management for their false accomplishment, no matter how unrealistic the goal of continuous improvement may be. Results of continuous improvement must be confirmed on the shop floor level by a method of analyzing the actual item in the actual location. Otherwise, continuous improvement can become superficial, especially for top management that is without immediate interest in solving the real issues.

Ohno enforced the principle of "Genchi Genbutsu" (Go and See) on a daily basis. He could immediately detect a forgery every time he had any doubt in the information he received. I could elaborate on this, as I have personally dealt with shop floors that tried to give me false information, but I will sum this up with the help of what Mr. Cho once said.

"If I reported "Hear-Say" information to Ohno without validating it by the principle of "Genchi Genbutsu," Ohno would never let me get away with it. Ohno was capable of determining the accuracy of a report by just hearing about it. Then, he would simply called us fools if we told him, honestly, that we had neglected seeing the shop floor first. If you experienced that once, you become hesitant to report to Ohno without a true understanding and investigation of our problems."

JUST OBSERVE THE SHOP FLOOR

Ohno was capable of not only determining if information was validated on the shop floor or not, he was also adept at detecting lies in the report itself. It was quite impressive to everyone. Ohno would receive piles of reports concerning the production performance of each factory every month. It was Ohno's idea to prepare such reports regularly so that any progress made in production over a certain period of time could be easily assessed. In most cases he stepped onto the shop floor before he asked any questions about such reports. He always observed the shop floor thoroughly and knew everything there was to know about production. With his keen eyes he immediately knew when some results did not seem to be a correct-fit for a certain shop floor environment.

Something new and unexpected can always be found if you step into the scene of a crime. For example, there are some cases in which production managers or team leaders choose to participate in a production line in order to boost efficiency so that a good report can be generated. However, it is not their responsibility to take part in a production line. Their role must be to stay outside of the production line so that they can constantly observe their workers and generate new continuous improvement ideas so that production efficiency can be increased exponentially. Consequently, such a report becomes doubtful because if those leaders fulfilled their responsibilities as they were supposed to, it is quite obvious that the production efficiency would not be as high as they claimed it to be.

As Ohno was a strong believer in the principle of "Genchi Genbutsu," he never approved of anything on paper unless appropriate judgments were made by studying the actual problems where they were occurring. If Ohno was presented only with documents and was persistently demanded to give his help based on them, he would say,

> "You are always on the shop floor therefore you know about the problem better than anyone else, including me. I cannot give you any answers because I have not seen the shop floor. When you are facing uncertainty or trying to come up with new ideas, just go back to the shop floor."

There are many expressions to remind us of the importance of the shop floor, such as "Diverse Shop Floors" and "The Sacred Shop Floor." However, nobody has ever understood the significance of the "Genchi Genbutsu" principle better than Ohno himself.

REASONING BEHIND THE TOYOTA SYSTEM

The advancement of IT in factories has required management staff to spend more time in performing data entry, as well as other conventional management duties. For this reason they often complain that they do not have enough time to visit the shop floor for problem-solving purposes. We must remember that nothing is more important than the shop floor and our effort should always be prioritized toward it. We must also impress into our minds that, as the Toyota System preaches, "You cannot bring the shop floor home with you."

Commandment 9

"Avoid labor enforcement. Humans can generate the best solutions for their own betterment."

DON'T DO WORK AT AN AVERAGE PACE; THE SHORTEST WAY IS ALWAYS THE EASIEST

ORDER OF CONTINUOUS IMPROVEMENT

Continuous improvement operates in a certain sequence, as follows:

(1) Operation Improvement

(2) Equipment Improvement

(3) Process Improvement

The Toyota System initiates continuous improvement by improving how its operations are handled. Instead of altering machinery or tools, the way work is performed is reexamined first so that better methods of operation can be reached with available resources. Then, it moves onto the next steps so that production efficiency and cost savings can increase by improving both machinery equipment and processes of manufacturing. One of the most important things to remember during this process is for us to pay enough attention so that new changes do not intensify the labor requirement for existing workers in any way.

The shop floor managers and continuous improvement promoters must observe their workers thoroughly while asking themselves such questions as "Are workers following standard work?", "Are they feeling stretched with their responsibilities?" and "Is their work simple enough?"

They must also take suggestions from the shop floor workers into consideration and formulate improvement ideas that are truly effective and beneficial to all. However, our continuous improvement ideas are not always as successful as we would hope and we will be faced with adverse effects, which are inevitable in some cases.

A young Toyota worker, Mr. V, completed an operation improvement strategy of his own and was feeling confident with the expected results. However, he learned that his idea was not working quite right on the shop floor. That is just the way of things, to a certain degree, as we cannot accept big changes easily. Even if a new way is scientifically proven to be more effective than our conventional way, we chose to stick with our old way only because we have grown accustomed to it.

New changes due to continuous improvement may turn out to be more time-consuming for workers, who will start questioning reasons why they were implemented in the first place. That is why we must understand the fact that new changes take time to be effectively adapted and have patience in explaining to workers the true purpose of such changes, in order to eliminate their discontent or fears of uncertainty.

Mr. V failed to do exactly that. Instead, when there was a

problem, he would step into the production line and show workers how it was supposed to be done, to yield the results based upon standard work. He would put pressure on his workers by saying, "Look, this is how you should be doing your work. Please learn my way as soon as possible."

Ohno saw Mr. V doing this one day and gave him a strict warning,

> "You've been so impatient in getting the results you demanded for. You did the work yourself and told workers to do it in your manner. You must think first of reasons why the results could not be yielded from the get-go. There must be an explanation why every worker is failing to accommodate your new strategy. Without discovering that by yourself, you're simply intensifying the labor requirement for your fellow workers. Show your respect toward them for a change!"

GRASP THE TRUE CAUSE OF AN ISSUE

First, it was obvious that Mr. V was incapable of getting positive results with the new method because he had formulated the method by trial and error. The shop floor workers were simply forced to accept the new method without receiving any proper explanations.

Secondly, Mr. V was not familiar with the old method, which the shop floor workers had been accustomed to doing their job for a long time. Thirdly, Mr. V did not have to perform the new method for as many hours as the shop floor workers did. He just tried a couple of times and told the workers that it was an easy thing to do. However, the shop floor workers would have to continue to adapt the new method on a daily basis for many months to come and suffer from certainty that the new method would lead to unfavorable results.

Mr. V believed that his new method would bring about

positive results that were never possible in the past, when in fact he was only demanding the shop floor workers to work harder. It was the same as labor enforcement after all.

Having received Ohno's advice, Mr. V recollected himself in an attempt to analyze the true cause for why his new method had failed to earn any acceptable outcomes. He visited the shop floor frequently and asked the workers to see if they had any concerns or demands. He found several issues with his method and eliminated them by conducting continuous improvement. Consequently, the operation began to run smoothly while generating steady progress toward achieving positive results.

Ohno's principle of "Respect for Workers" is rooted in grasping the true cause of a problem and formulating a continuous improvement measure to eliminate such causes. It is also the basis for avoiding any labor enforcement upon existing workers. For example, when a standard work time is to be determined, many factories choose to calculate an average processing time and use that to draw a reasonable standard work time for a certain task. Ohno despised this method and often said,

> "A standard work time should be the shortest processing time you have ever achieved."

This may sound like an implication of labor enforcement but the true purpose of his doctrine was something else. If the same task is performed 10 times, it does not mean that it is performed in the exact same manner every time. Therefore, Ohno strongly believed that the shortest processing time can only be achieved by eliminating errors and wastes entirely and is the most efficient and simplest way of performing work.

That is why a standard work time should be based on the shortest processing time. However, this is only effective under one condition; we must not simply order workers to try harder to get accustomed to new ways. It is our responsibility to break down the true cause for why the standard work times are not being met and guide workers through so that they become fully capable of eliminating problems by themselves.

REASONING BEHIND THE TOYOTA SYSTEM

Always ask yourself "Why?" repeatedly while observing the shop floor in detail. Ask questions like, "Why is work performed in a certain way?", "Why are workers moving in a wasteful manner?" and "Why are we having trouble reducing standard work time?" Then, start thinking firmly about what you can do to improve the situation. A "Can-Do" attitude is only a form of ambition, not necessarily a solution.

CONTINUOUSLY IMPROVE ON A PATTERN OF FAILURE DO THE SAME FOR A PATTERN OF SUCCESS

DON'T JUST DIAGNOSE PROBLEMS, CURE THEM

"Your job is not only to diagnose a problem, but also to treat it with a cure."

Ohno used to tell that to young Toyota workers. It is easy enough to visit the shop floor and only point out wastes. If you have a certain amount of knowledge and experience, you are more than likely able to indicate 10 or 20 categories of waste immediately. However, this is only a diagnosis of visual problems. It is a whole new level to go beyond that and conceive solutions in order to eliminate such wastes and solve bigger issues.

We must remember that the essential goal of continuous improvement is to achieve a total optimization of production. We must also acknowledge that continuous improvements that fix problems in a certain process can simultaneously cause adverse effects, such as an increase in cost or decrease in performance efficiency, on the overall production system. This type of improvement is obviously pointless. The efficiency of each process must be improved with much consideration toward that of the entire production system.

In addition, not all of the continuous improvement techniques created by Toyota are applicable to other factories. Continuous improvement can become continuous degradation unless we start customizing such techniques according to the size of each company, category of industry that the company belongs to, as well as the quality and skill of its workers. By doing so you can develop a cure for the shop floor.

As Ohno strongly believed, the shop floor starts to see improvement only when a cure is found. There are also different levels and categories of cures, such as cures for equipment and processes, as well as ultimate cures, which are designed to boost the production of an entire factory while reducing production cost. Ohno used to tell his subordinates to start by applying small cures and gradually work their way up to a higher level. Ultimately, Ohno would tell his subordinates, "Overhaul that factory and boost its profitability." This was usually a sign of reaching the highest level of management cure, so to speak.

GO HELP OTHER COMPANIES GENERATE PROFITS

In the late 1950's Mr. W was sent to an affiliate company that was experiencing a business slump. Mr. W had gained extensive experience under Ohno assisting various production reforms in many affiliate companies in the past. In some cases, he would become a resident of an affiliate company for several months and promote changes until a substantial result was obtained, then he would return to Toyota.

In most cases, his responsibilities were mainly oriented toward technical improvement, however it was for something else this time around. Ohno sent Mr. W by saying,

> "I want you to understand that you are not going there for technical assistance and training this time. Your job is to run the company, which means that you will have to lead them

to profits. Your job is not completed until the company is reformed to accommodate that. I am counting on you."

Mr. W definitely had enough experience and confidence in improving companies to reduce production costs and, in fact, he had proven his capacity of yielding profits in production departments in many cases. However, Ohno's order concerned not only the factory but the company as a whole. It was not only a matter of the production department, it was relevant to all of the existing departments which would be required to join together toward the same goal. Mr. W was not sure he could pull this off at first but made a commitment to realizing Ohno's request.

The company to which Mr. W was transferred had managed to maintain a low rate of profitability, however they had a tendency to remain in debt and employ a relatively large number of workers, in spite of their weak sales. Reducing the number of workers is the simplest and easiest way to cut down production costs, however Mr. W was sternly ordered by Ohno to "not lay off employees unless it is absolutely the only way."

Mr. W thought that the only way to promise profits was to reduce the actual cost of production by carrying out a stringent production reform. His idea was to implement the Toyota System in the entire factory. However, the company was reluctant to do so at once because a large portion of business was still taking place with non-Toyota customers. Mr. W decided to limit applying the Toyota System to only the items that were supplied to Toyota and see what would happen. It was a success to do so, however there were other problems.

The problems were with the suppliers that provided the company with essential components and raw materials for production. Mr. W demanded the company eliminate inventories and demand that its suppliers implement a "Just-In-Time" system. However, the company strongly desired to stock up items in advance in order to maintain their conventional mass production system. Mr. W visited each supplier and provided technical assistance in order to assist their understanding of "Just-In-Time" and an ability to accept new changes.

After one year, as far as Toyota-related components were concerned, the company, as well as its suppliers, succeeded in adopting the Toyota System into their operations. Although it took a long time the company eventually reformed the entire operation, which led to a substantial cost reduction while securing profits at all times.

Ohno's way of training his proteges always started by giving them easily-attainable goals first and gradually challenging them to obtain more difficult goals. Ohno would ask for small continuous improvement in the beginning and eventually put the fate of a company in their hands. The episode of Mr. W is a good example. The future and profitability of the company was heavily dependant on his accomplishment. At the same time, Ohno would tell them,

"Solve the problem upon discovering it."

It is far from being over after you make a report such as saying, "This kind of a waste exists" or "That kind of a problem exists." A solution must be formulated and applied to the problem immediately. Ohno would always ask if an improvement made in a certain process was successfully carried over to other processes so that a comprehensive betterment of the entire process could be achieved. Ohno believed that this was the only method to boost the work efficiency without intensifying labor resources. It may be true to say that the reason why Ohno said to his proteges, "The job is not done until a substantial profit is promised" was to show his trust and acceptance for their great leadership.

REASONING BEHIND THE TOYOTA SYSTEM

A medical treatment cannot be called what it is if patients were only diagnosed. It must make sure that patients are fully healed after proper recovery and rehabilitation processes. In the same sense, we must start from generating small improvements one at a time, after identifying problems, and direct ourselves to achieving more substantial results in order to be true to continuous improvement.

Avoid setting goals too high because that takes away the confidence of workers and their willingness to try will be deteriorated. The important thing is to achieve time-proven strategies one by one and gradually challenge even the highest level of improvement.

THE STARTING POINT CAN BE LOW AS LONG AS YOUR GOAL IS SET HIGH

IMPRACTICAL PRINCIPLES ARE USELESS

It is a Toyota doctrine that "Continuous improvement can only be built upon standards." It is meaningless to change the way work is performed on the shop floor in a place where everyone has his own ideas and way of doing the job. This is because there is not a set of standards to compare against. Even continuous improvement ideas are not applicable to such a shop floor environment. This is why standard work must be created.

The Toyota System has preached that standard work must be created by the shop floor workers. In many companies, it is the managers who determine standard work and orders their workers to work according to job manuals. However, this method will create resentment among workers, unless they are fully involved in deciding what the standard work should be. It is often far from being respectful to workers and considered an ineffective tool for promoting continuous improvement.

I remember Ohno telling me the following episode,

> "I think it was 1933 or 1934, when I was working in the Toyota textile factory, that I was told by my supervisor to create a standard work manual. I tried to find some reference books in the bookstore but I had absolutely no luck in

coming up with any useful information. At the time, every standard work manual tended to be quite idealistic. Mine turned out like that too. It was so unrealistic that no one on the shop floor was able to follow it."

Ohno reflected on his own experiences and gave us guidance as to how a standard work should be established and applied to real practices.

"No matter how great the principles behind a manual are, it has no value if it cannot be applied in practice. We're not living in an ivory tower. Work can never be standardized based only upon your ideas and demands without validating facts on the shop floor. Focus on one problem at a time and try to accomplish continuous improvement no matter how small it may be. This is how you can collect useful clues as to what standard work should be."

As Ohno described, the following three points are extremely important in establishing standard work:

(1) The reality of the shop floor is clearly reflected in standard work.

(2) Standard work must be realistic and applicable to the shop floor.

(3) Standard work must lead to continuous improvement opportunities.

These are the main reason why Ohno demanded the shop floor workers must decide on standard work. In doing that, he also reminded workers that their idea of standard work did not always have to be substantial to begin with.

"It's wrong to think that you need to fabricate your own standard work idea only because it is being compared to ones made by others. Impressive standard work is never absolute in practice. First, pick a starting point that fits you the best and create a solid foundation which will help you gather useful clues for establishing a more desirable and attainable achievement of standard work," he said.

This pretty much sums up Ohno's unique approach.

PERFECTION IS NOT YOUR DESTINATION

Humans have a strong tendency to seek perfection when creating manuals, including standard work. A few months can easily fly by while we brainstorm for such manuals. Ohno thought it was ridiculous to spend that much time for creating a manual and often scolded his workers for that. His workers were instead advised to focus on figuring out how work should be done in practice on the shop floor. Ohno demanded managers constantly revise their manuals and change how work had to be performed accordingly as he said,

> "Standard work must be continuously improved... for eternity."

A standard work manual should hang on the wall with the date of compilation on it, for example. Managers observe how workers are performing their work and promote continuous improvement strategies to make their work simpler and more efficient, while listening to their suggestions and complaints about the existing methods. Standard work manuals should be updated immediately after positive and more effective results are achieved by the hands of the shop floor workers.

In reality, standard work manuals get updated quite infrequently in a shop floor where workers are actively engaged in continuous improvement. As a result, older versions of the manual were still left hanging on the wall to a point where their pages had been discolored from the length of time they had been there.

Ohno would see this and ask the shop floor

managers, "You have been getting paid for doing nothing. Have you not been working at all this past month?"

This sounds like a pretty harsh remark. However, it was Ohno's unique and sincere way to constantly remind managers that their responsibilities were rooted deeply in making sure that continuous improvements actually take place on the shop floor level. He also strongly believed that standard work had to be generated on the shop floor level and improved on a daily basis, which would eventually establish a creative climate of continuous improvement in every worker.

Ohno used to say the following in regard to standard work, "Do not aim for perfection. Create a lenient standard work to begin with."

Even for continuous improvement ideas, if they were perfectly formulated to begin with, workers would be less likely to generate their own ideas in order to help such ideas become absolute. Ohno believed that creating standard work is the same way as well. If they were made with room for improvement, workers would surely contribute their own solutions and suggestions toward establishing more sophisticated versions of standard work.

REASONING BEHIND THE TOYOTA SYSTEM

An environment where workers can easily contribute their new ideas can be created by purposefully keeping them challenged and even giving them hardship. Such an environment helps workers feel remarkably satisfied for utilizing their own intelligence and craftiness, especially when such ideas bring out immediate or long-term results. It is like a pump-priming method. Various methods and mechanisms must also be considered so that a climate where worker's ideas are always encouraged can be established.

Decisions can be based on profitability, but that shouldn't be the only factor

DO NOT INSTALL NEW ROBOTS BASED ON THEIR POPULARITY

Robotization of production has become essential to a certain degree and remains quite challenging for us at the present day, just as it did in the past. A few years ago, the manager of a company visited the Toyota factory and sighed with grief to realize how modern the robots were in Toyota compared to those in his own factory. His company was quite active in adapting new robots in production, however it had failed to increase operation efficiency on the shop floor and decrease production costs, as expected, in spite of the new robots. On the other hand, Toyota had succeeded where his company did not after adapting various kinds of robots.

The manager asked Toyota about how robots were adapted differently in Toyota and started to see some obvious reasons why. As far as Toyota factories are concerned, they follow these steps when they replace existing robots with new ones:

(1) Replace existing robots with human workers and perform the same process.

(2) Workers eliminate wastes completely in the process and develop continuous improvement strategies.

(3) After a confirmation is made that new robots can be adapted into a new environment without any issues, development of new robots is initiated.

(4) Company-specific specifications of new robots are formulated in the industrial technology and production development.

(5) Seek continuous improvement on a daily

basis after new robots begin operating on the shop floor.

In the manager's factory, on the other hand, new robots were installed by third-party vendors without conducting enough discussions. The shop floor workers often did not see any room for their ideas with these new robots and therefore chose not to participate in continuous improvement activities after the installation. They also simply replaced robots according to their expiration dates.

The manager noticed these obvious reasons why Toyota always succeeded and started focusing on acquiring continuous improvement little by little, so that only essential robots were introduced to production with a promising outcome.

Ohno used to say, in regards to this matter, "Don't install new robots based on their popularity." When Ohno used to visit suppliers, he would sometimes find cutting-edge robots running in production in spite of their relatively small factory sizes.

> "Don't you think it makes sense for your factory to have these superior machines?" he would ask.

> "We need to have these machines to impress people these days so that they want to work in our facility," the factory managers would reply.

The assumption was that an absence of modern machinery often gave people false impressions that the factory could be falling behind other factories. It would also detract people from wanting to work in such a factory and influence customers to make decisions of conducting business, under the same such assumptions. Ohno strongly resented this type of attitude, for it was only superficial, and these factories then failed to take into consideration any changes in production cost.

The most important thing here is that an adaptation of new robots must always achieve reduction in production costs. New robots should be implemented only after the existing equipment has been continuously improved to a point that further improvement is no longer possible and future reduction in production cost becomes possible only by an installation of new robots.

DON'T BECOME A GUARDIAN FOR MACHINERY

Ohno stressed that we should never part with our respect toward existing workers in the process of adapting new robots into production. When someone told Ohno "This robot can eliminate three workers," Ohno responded by saying, "What are those three workers supposed to do after losing their positions?" It would not be a problem if those three workers had some other skills and continued to add value to production, however this is not always the case. If there is nothing else they can contribute themselves to, installing new robots would simply add extra cost to production.

Terminating those workers is not a solution either. Otherwise robotization would become a bully toward workers who are capable of performing only a certain type of task. If new robots were the only available method of surviving a crisis, it would be acceptable, but it is usually just an insult toward technically-challenged workers. Ohno would warn us about this issue on a frequent basis.

There is another thing concerning robotization that we need to be careful of. We must not continue to use existing workers to perform hazardous tasks in order to avoid absorbing the high costs that are associated with purchasing new robots. This seems like common sense to us, however some factories have actually done exactly that. For tasks that are innately dangerous or of sanitary concerns an increased cost of production due to installing new robots can be justified, to a reasonably degree. At any rate, Ohno hated the attitude of depreciating the true value of human workers and assigning them simply as guardians to machinery.

REASONING BEHIND THE TOYOTA SYSTEM

The purpose of robotization, computerization, and automation is essentially to make our lives easier and more meaningful. Any adaptation of such mechanisms without respect to human potential will result in serious overburdening in one form or another. Any changes or improvement in the shop floor environment must center themselves around our respect to human beings at all times.

Commandment 10

"Customer criticism is the gateway to our success. Use it to your advantage by formulating solutions."

CHANGE YOURSELF FIRST IF YOU WANT TO CHANGE SOMEONE ELSE

WHY ASK OUR SUPPLIERS TO MANUFACTURE ITEMS THAT WE CAN PRODUCE ON OUR OWN?

Deciding what items should be outsourced or self-manufactured is a critical factor in determining how much profit can be made. If only profits are concerned, both cumbersome and inexpensive items should be actively purchased by sub-contracting with suppliers that deliver items by "Just-In-Time." When Ohno became fully in charge of the production management department, Toyota was following that particular way of decision making process and prioritizing its own profits.

Mr. X was working in the head office of purchasing and followed the same principle. Ohno would ask Mr. X "How are you ever going to succeed?" and criticized Mr. X's actions on two points.

The first point pertained to limited subcontracts. Limited subcontracts entail short-term outsourcing of certain products that are found to be a challenge due to the temporal lack of resources that are required to produce such items by self-manufacturing. A limited subcontract lasts for one to two months on average and expires when the company regains its capacity to manufacture the items by themselves. It was an extremely convenient method to supplement production and was used as a common practice by Toyota at that time. When Mr. X asked Ohno's advice on sub-contracting certain items in this manner, he was reprimanded.

> "Why are you doing such a meaningless thing? Outsourced factories go through so much hassle just to prepare themselves with sufficient labor and equipment for accommodating our orders, even if it's just for a month. What do you think would happen to those factories if our orders were cancelled after such a short period of time? Once you make a decision to outsource certain items, you must be fully determined that those items will continue to be outsourced and will not be returned so that we can produce them on our own," Ohno declared.

Mr. X had no idea why Ohno was so angry. He thought that limited subcontracts provided great opportunities to the suppliers and that it was not Toyota's business to worry about them losing orders after a short time. Without Mr. X fully understanding the reasons why, Ohno put an end to practicing limited subcontracts from then on.

The second point regarded subcontracts other than limited subcontracts. It was a common practice back then to self-manufacture large-quantity items and outsource items that were complex and in small quantities. However, Ohno thought of doing exactly the opposite. He would say to everyone,

"Small-quantity items should be self-manu-factured. On the other hand, mass-produced items that are inexpensive and easy to produce should be outsourced. I'm aware that it is costly to self-manufacture small-quantity items, how-ever that can be justified as it will inspire us to challenge reducing our own cost by practicing continuous improvement."

Disciplining mechanism

Ohno said to Mr. X, who had always thought that out-sourcing small-quantity items was beneficial in order to run in-house mass production processes more smoothly,

"You are outsourcing items that Toyota failed to produce with success and expecting that our suppliers will be able to do a better job than we did. If such suppliers exist, you should be begging them to teach us how. Of course, your salary would be lower than that of workers at such suppliers."

DO NOT IMPOSE RISKS OUTSIDE OF YOUR COMPANY

The biggest challenge that Kiichiro had faced in found-ing Toyota Motor Industry was to establish and cultivate a strong network of component suppliers, which were quite scarce in Japanese industry at the time. Therefore, Toyota acknowledged the importance of coexisting and yielding mutual benefits with its suppliers under ordinary circum-stances. However, Toyota also subconsciously suffered from its tendency to prioritize its own benefit by taking advantage of their suppliers. Ohno never allowed this type of attitude as it seriously jeopardized their healthy relationships.

Mr. X began to understand what Ohno was trying to convey to him. To Ohno, every process in production ex-isted on a continuum, no matter if it was by suppliers in the beginning or Toyota that conducted the final assem-bly. If even a small part of the continuum was weakened, that meant that the final product would never be of good quality and could not be produced at a reasonable cost in a timely fashion. This is why Ohno believed in the importance of self-manufacturing the most challenging items and passing on newly acquired knowledge and techniques to suppliers for their future development.

This would eventually lead to various continuous improvement ideas within Toyota, which could be carried over to a supplier level as well. After all, this strategy would yield the same results as a total optimization of production would, so Toyota itself could greatly benefit from it in the long run.

This thinking was not limited to Ohno. Eiji Toyoda also commanded his workers to do this, who would otherwise easily avoid the challenge by outsourcing instead of self-manufacturing.

Challenging work always imposes risks. Eiji refused to impose such risks upon third-party suppliers and shared the sense of crisis that a lack of in-house technical advantages, for overcoming such risks, could lead to much more serious consequences in the end.

As Ohno preached persistently, the Toyota System strives to accommodate self-manufacturing as much as it possibly can. Outsourcing is permitted only after it is proven that the same outsourced production can be carried out in its own factories. As a result inconsiderate outsourcing to suppliers can be successfully avoided.

Even though Mr. X had been aware of the significant role that suppliers played in production on a larger scale, he failed to respect that in practice. Thus he became oblivious to the inconvenience to suppliers, being so fixated upon Toyota's own profits.

Once he learned this important lesson from Ohno, he began conducting his work by first reminding himself, "Someday our suppliers will begin recognizing us as a true business partner, instead of us simply categorizing them as a partner."

REASONING BEHIND THE TOYOTA SYSTEM

The Toyota System refers to earlier processes as Gods and later processes as Patrons. Earlier processes include suppliers. They act like Gods because they provide us with items that we could not produce by ourselves otherwise. On the other hand, later processes should never receive any defects and must be treated in the same way we treat our patrons. Never pass on defects, not just to end-users but to your fellow processes, because they too are customers.

ASK WORKERS TO DO HARD THINGS IN A GENTLE MANNER; ASK WORKERS TO DO EASY THINGS REPEATEDLY

HOW TO PREPARE WORKERS FOR THE WORST

The Toyota System not only sets high expectations for suppliers in terms of purchasing price, delivery cycle and the shop floor environment, but also provides sufficient technical and financial assistance so that suppliers can meet those expectations at all times. Toyota workers may also be dispatched to give technical support for a substantial time period. Such Toyota technicians were expected to have a strong commitment toward success and be prepared for the worst during the time when Ohno was in charge of cultivating trust between Toyota and its suppliers.

At one point a Toyota supplier, in charge of producing auto body frames, was not meeting the quality standard and was falling behind its quota. This was a serious issue as it affected the entire post production process. Ohno assigned young Toyota worker Mr. Y to solve the problem on site. Ohno simply told him, "Go and put everything back to normal."

Mr. Y visited the supplier and observed the dismal performance of the shop floor workers, even though they were trying their best and were working as late as 11pm every night. As he was under strict orders from Ohno, he had to try everything he could to improve the situation.

Mr. Y requested Ohno dispatch a team of 5 experienced Toyota engineers and initiated continuous improvement activities with the team. The shop floor was starting to see remarkable progress, however Mr. Y wanted to get the help of one more engineer to achieve his goal. He tried getting a hold of his supervisor by phone, to make the request for one more engineer to be sent in.

Ohno happened to be the one to pick up the phone when Mr. Y called in. Mr. Y told Ohno that the shop floor had been improved and that one more engineer was needed to derive further results by continuous improvement. Ohno did not approve the request and told Mr. Y's supervisor that Mr. Y was just complaining instead of trying harder. Mr. Y interpreted Ohno's reaction as being told he had to pull it off with only the available resources, no matter what.

Mr. Y also had no prior experiences in negotiating with labor unions on his own and, what was worse, was that this company had maintained a strong labor union. Every time he requested changes in the existing working condition he was confronted with resistance. The labor union continuously protested, saying that it was a form of labor enforcement. He had to go through a long process to persuade the union otherwise.

Mr. Y had found it cumbersome at first, however he had prepared for the worst case scenario and committed himself to explaining the top management executives of the company, with confidence, why new changes were needed and how they were better than their old ways.

He also changed the way he dealt with the shop floor. In the past, he was over-confident about himself for being an elite from Toyota and just gave his orders to workers on the shop floor and walked away. He made it his habit to stay on the shop floor and maintained open communications with workers, which created an environment where everyone could share new ideas and concerns easily. This type of teamwork was persistent throughout the day until production ended, around 10pm, on a daily basis.

IMPORTANCE OF COLLABORATIVE EFFORTS

Collaborative effort with the shop floor workers was the major contributor to Mr. Y's success. The shop floor workers would not get motivated if some superior only showed up every once in a while and told them what to do. Such a superior, who is never on the shop floor but always in his office usually gets reports from the shop floor supervisor and simply gives out a new set of orders to follow.

Mr. Y tried to do it differently and succeeded. He would show up on the shop floor frequently and got involved in the problem-solving and idea generating processes with the workers. If his workers had to work overtime, he was always there to support them.

It is true to say that everyone was suspicious of him in the beginning, as they normally were toward outside superiors. However, everyone clearly observed his enthusiasm and began to cooperate by proactively generating their new ideas and continuous improvement activities took off during this time.

He did not go back to Toyota at all during this time and stayed in a nearby hotel to commute directly to the company. After a couple months the framework for his goal was established and he began to think about going back to Toyota.

As illustrated in this episode, Ohno never gave his dispatched representatives any deadlines, nor did he tell them when they could return from their missions. Ohno implied by this that goals had to be achieved with no exceptions and that they could only return when they became confident with the end results. Dispatched representatives could not show their incompetence or complain to Ohno as he would simply call it whining. They had to achieve their mission no matter what, and how much time, it took.

A few years later Mr. Y was appointed as the President of a company and succeeded in returning profitability to it within a three year period. This was accomplished by his collaborative effort with the shop floor workers in reforming the entire production mechanism based on the principles of the Toyota System. To achieve the same result across the board, he actively dispatched his technicians, who were leaders in the reform, to suppliers so that their production systems were improved as well.

Even though his dispatches were only for a short time, usually one to two weeks, and were not as extensive as those done by Ohno, he strongly believed that it would still be a remarkable learning opportunity for his young subordinates to work in other companies with different corporate cultures. Mr. Y once told me,

> "Any significant reforms within your own company can overcome conflicts and resistance and lead to mutual understanding because it is done among people who share the same corporate identity and way of thinking. However, it's challenging to promote any changes in a company that has a different corporate culture than the one you are accustomed to. I intentionally send my subordinates, especially the young ones, to such companies. I know it's a harsh way of learning for them but I believe that it is the most effective way for them to grow as true leaders. Remove them from the comfort of their own houses and let them suffer the hardship of life for a change."

REASONING BEHIND THE TOYOTA SYSTEM

A human being can be considered fully-fledged only after he becomes capable of winning a battle against those who possess different styles and traditions. It is also true to say that fighting with one's back to the wall is the only way to grow as a leader. Mr. Cho once optimistically said,

> "Because Ohno trained me very well in his own unique way I can now take on any challenge of helping a company get on their feet, at anytime, with no hassles."

AN "I CAN" CONVICTION CAN BE AS DEDICATED AS AN "I CAN'T" CONVICTION

YOUR OPPOSITION CAN BECOME YOUR STRONGEST SUPPORTER IF TRUTHFULLY COMMUNICATED WITH

One of the biggest challenges and obstacles in advocating production reform is to acquire enough cooperation from a network of suppliers. Suppliers can also provide us with support, such as delivering components by a "Just-In-Time" system, while establishing strict standards for how they are packaged. In some cases, suppliers are asked to alter the design of certain components for more efficiency and participate in formulating new ideas jointly in order to deliver better quality items in a less expensive way. Such collaborative efforts bring mutual advantages to both your company and suppliers. However, it is not that easy in reality. Many suppliers refuse to cooperate and are difficult to persuade.

When a young Toyota worker, Mr. Z, was dispatched by Ohno to promote the Toyota System among suppliers and partner companies, he was brought to a standstill when dealing with the high level of resistance from the president of a partner company. The company held a large volume of inventory, as its business had been based on mass production for many years. They would deliver items from stock in inventory as orders came in. Received orders could have been filled easily by conducting a high-variety low-volume manufacturing process, however they chose to produce each item in lot by mass production, which led to more excessive inventories.

This was the main concern of Mr. Z, who attempted to convince the production management team to adopt the Toyota System for the purpose of reducing inventories. After the production manager fully comprehended the true benefits of the Toyota System by all possible means, including touring of many Toyota factories, he made a suggestion to the president. However, the president refused to even listen to the production manager and maintained his opposition against the Toyota System.

Mr. Z explained the situation to Ohno and asked for his advice as to what should be done to earn the president's approval.

> "The president must be showing resistance because of his own convictions. There's nothing wrong with that. However, it is wrong for you to make a judgment without learning his reasons. He must have his own strong beliefs and logics toward how his company should be run. Instead of convincing him of your idea, learn from such an unbreakable dedication to his own principles," Ohno said.

What Ohno meant was that both the president and Mr. Z acted in accordance with their beliefs. By understanding that, Mr. Z would be able to eventually persuade the president by paying full attention to the opinions of the president and challenging the president's beliefs, while keeping the faith in his own beliefs at the same time.

Ohno's advice encouraged Mr. Z to visit the president repeatedly in the hope of convincing him that the change was absolutely necessary and promising the president that he would commit himself to achieving great success in the end. Consequently, Mr. Z began to understand the reason why the president was being reluctant.

The company had conducted business with Toyota for many years, during which time his company never caused any troubles to Toyota by not failing to provide the necessary items in time, something the president was very proud of. He was aware that mass production continued to result in excessive inventories, as his factory received orders that were mostly for many models in small quantities. However, he would not accept any changes in the existing system in order to avoid a serious risk of running out of inventories, which could be quite troublesome to Toyota.

Therefore, it is true to judge that his decision against the suggested production reform arose from his dedication toward the healthy relationship between Toyota and his company. Mr. Z managed to persuade the president by promising him that the reform would not lead to any problems, including shortages of inventories, and began moving forward with the cooperation from the company staff. It was observed by everyone that the Toyota System began to reduce the volume of inventories significantly and prepare the factory for accommodating Build-to-Order manufacturing instead.

In the beginning, both the president and the shop floor workers were concerned with the inventories running out. However, they were able to eliminate such concerns by gaining progress, little by little, by practicing continuous improvement, which eventually led to a successful reform without any serious complications.

Mr. Z performed an extremely hard task, both in persuading the president and providing endless assistance to accomplishing the goals of the reform. Working closely together with the president and staff toward the goals enabled him to establish a solid relationship of mutual trust with the company. The biggest achievement of all was that the company transformed itself to a point where it was able to return stable profitability and become proficient in generating continuous improvement.

Mr. Z learned through this experience that persuading a person of strong conviction was a challenging thing to do. However, a mutual understanding could be gained as long as he challenged it with his own conviction. He also acknowledged that such a person could be much more understanding and supportive, once persuaded, than anyone else.

THE IMPORTANCE OF CONVICTION IN YOUR OWN BELIEFS

If I were to describe Ohno in one phrase, it would be "person of conviction." When Ohno first introduced the Toyota System, the shop floor workers viewed it as a form of labor enforcement, even though it was approved of by Ishida Taizo and Eiji Toyoda. Ohno received much criti-

Implies that a discrete form of production was comprehended and approved.

cism as the Toyota System was also believed to have denied everything they worked for in the past entirely. Workers would say things like "If we followed Ohno, our company would go bankrupt," and demanded Eiji Toyoda fire him immediately.

Ohno once said the following in regards to the criticism he had received,

> "I had many complaints and concerns from workers that my ideas could lead to a serious disaster for Toyota. I was thinking the same toward those people. If we continued to do their old way of production, we would go bankrupt for sure."

The shop floor workers had their conviction in their old way of production while Ohno had his conviction in promoting changes for future survival. By bringing his conviction face to face with theirs and persuading the workers of the true virtue of his ideas Ohno won the battle and established the Toyota System firmly in place. Anyone could have come up with the principles of the Toyota System, per se, however nobody could have realized them with stronger intentions and convictions than Ohno did.

REASONING BEHIND THE TOYOTA SYSTEM

> Eiji Toyoda once said, "Anyone can design new mechanisms on a piece of paper. However, the most critical thing is how much of such principles can actually be carried out in practice."

Real work should not be done only in your head. Our ideas begin adding true value to work only when they are realized with our strong conviction and determination.

MAKE A GREAT TEAM AND CONTINUOUSLY IMPROVE IT

TEAMWORK IS EVERYTHING

One thing that Toyota Motors has taken seriously in recent years is effective communication among workers who are on the same level, as well as in the relationship between superiors and subordinates. Toyota has revised, from scratch, how each of their workers is communicated with in the belief that allowing effective and open communication among their workers is the key to building a strong shop floor.

In the past, the shop floor workers were supervised in groups of 10 by a manager. However, this was found to be too large of a group to pay enough attention to each worker. Nowadays, a supervisor manages groups of only 5 workers so that everybody receives enough attention.

There has been a tendency in Toyota that individual achievement is being valued more than collective effort. At the same time, Toyota has experienced many different types of employment other than traditional full-time employees. These include those who are outsourced and contracted part-time as well as those dispatched from sister companies to provide Toyota with technical assistant for a limited period of time.

These factors have made it challenging for Toyota to unify workers. This is the main reason why Toyota reviewed its working team structure and set a goal for treating each worker as a respectful individual by maintaining close interactions at all times. One of the unique characteristics of this endeavor is that the revision of its working team structure is also aimed toward workers other than full-time employees.

From the beginning, Ohno emphasized that "teamwork is everything" when it came to implementing the Toyota System in production. He also used the following analogy:

"When you think of a boat rowed by eight athletes or a baseball game played by two teams of nine players, the outcome of such a game is heavily dependant upon teamwork. You'll never be able to win against the competition if you only have one or two star players in your team. That is the ironic part. Production in my factories is carried out in teams. In one process, we have as many as 10 to 15 workers working together while sharing responsibilities to complete the job. Therefore, teamwork becomes the most important factor in achieving success. The real question isn't about how many items each worker processed or punched holes in, but is about how many finished items that each team has completed collectively at the end."

TAKE ADVANTAGE OF THE BATON PASSING ZONE

Another one of Ohno's sayings was "Take advantage of the baton passing zone." He was referring to a relay race in which a special zone is designated for athletes to pass a baton during the race. The outcome of a relay race is determined by how well athletes perform this task. If they fail to do it well even a strong team could still lose the race, no matter how fast each runner is by himself. Ohno believed that the same principle was applicable to work.

When working at a process in a team environment, items can be considered as a baton. For example, if a worker in the later process is falling behind, you can help him catch up with his work, like performing his changeover responsibility for him, and make sure he is back on track before a baton is handed over to him. Why is this kind of care necessary?

As far as work or sports are concerned, it would be ideal if everyone playing in a team had equal strength and capabilities, however that is not a possibility in reality. There are differences in the productivity of each worker, as new employees and contracted short-term workers have to be taken into consideration. Consequently, such differences are mitigated by the principle of "Baton Passing," which was often referred to as a "collaborate effort campaign." Ohno strongly believed that such a campaign could nourish each worker and create stronger teamwork.

In a campaign of promoting closer communications and stronger teamwork among workers there is one thing that must be avoided, which is the creation of "remote islands" on the shop floor. Rationalization of production causes the number of workers to go down. Reduction in excessive labor is equally important, however this can create a shop floor where both workers and machinery are placed sparsely about, like remote islands. It also prevents workers from working closely together as a team. If a worker is performing his job in isolation, Ohno suggested that such a worker ought to be brought together with other workers with the same responsibility so that teamwork could be maintained.

I have personally been exposed to the adverse effect of these remote islands in a certain company. The company was relatively large in size and its production lines stretched out extremely long as well. Items were being processed on the first floor and transported to the second floor for the later process. After it had been completed, the items were transported back onto the first floor. On top of that, there were only a small number of workers in the factory. Workers were being assigned to large machines located further apart from one another, on both the first and second floor, which created a number of remote islands throughout the shop floor.

What is the consequence of this? For example, say defects were discovered in a certain process. The Toyota System would immediately stop production and eliminate such defects by identifying the true cause. However, if workers had to travel a great distance between earlier and later processes, like traveling either to the first floor or second floor in my example, workers would find it cumbersome to deal with defects immediately and defects would eventually be forgotten.

Under ordinary circumstances it is not desirable for workers to act this way, however it is merely human nature. In these cases, neither a "collective effort campaign" nor close communication with the shop floor were expected to take place, as workers became unable to casually interact with other workers in both the earlier and later processes.

A production reform, based on the Toyota System, was introduced to the factory and as a result the issues associated with "remote islands" were gradually eliminated. This was done by placing production lines on the same floor and moving workstations closer to one another.

This was an experience that reminded me once again of the serious consequences associated with placing workers on the shop floor without a specific plan and the importance of creating a work environment where close communication among workers was always possible. I strongly believe that our work cannot yield progress without embracing and encouraging human-to-human interactions. Therefore, we must place the greatest importance on encouraging close and effective communication and supporting the collaborative effort of all the workers.

REASONING BEHIND THE TOYOTA SYSTEM

We must always look for not only physical but also invisible distances and walls that influence the performance of each worker. Healthy communication always leads to a higher quality of work and teamwork, which positively empowers the shop floor in the long run.

Afterword

The creators of the Toyota Production System, Kiichiro Toyoda and Taiichi Ohno, had many things in common. The biggest commonality was their commitment to not only theorizing their ideas, but bringing them to life.

When new changes are introduced, strong conflicts or resistance to such changes comes with the territory and many leaders can easily be turned off by that. Both Kiichiro and Ohno's strong faith in themselves and unwavering convictions toward delivering positive results have contributed to the successful implementation and development of the Toyota Production System.

In recent years the Toyota System has been popularized among many types of industries. Even in these new industries resistance and opposition to change are still inevitable. In order for implementation to be successful, resistance must be dealt with by a strong dedication to the process.

The 10 Commandments of Ohno that I have described in this book are not just theories for your mind, they are extremely important guidances based on the words and practices of Taiichi Ohno. These guidances can lead to solid preparedness and effective techniques that are essential for those determined for improvement. Use them as a road map for promoting breakthroughs in your company, as guidelines to bring about new changes, for overcoming your own hesitation, and also to deal with resistances from others.

Remember, anyone can come up with ideas. It is up to you to nurture and help bring forth tangible results because of those ideas.

I will be honored to see my book helping the readers rediscover that the most important achievement is the ability to carry out your ideas with great confidence and success.

Index

B

C

D

I

J

K

L

M

S

T

U

Publications from Enna

From Enna's new classics by Shigeo Shingo to our Lean Origin Series, Enna provides companies with the foundation of knowledge and practical implementation ideas that will ensure your efforts to internalize process improvement. Reach your vision and mission with the expertise within these world-class texts. Call toll-free (866) 249-7348 or visit us on the web at www.enna.com to order or request our free product catalog.

Mistaken Kanbans

Let Mistaken Kanbans be your roadmap to guide you through the steps necessary to implement and successful Kanban System. This book will help you to not only understand the complexities of a Kanban System but gives you the tools necessary, and the guidance through real-life lessons learned, to avoid disasterous consequences related to the improper use of such systems.

ISBN 978-1-926537-10-8 | 2009 | $27.99 | Item: 919

The Toyota Way in Sales and Marketing

Many companies today are trying to implement the ideas and principles of Lean into non-traditional environments, such as service centers, sales organizations and transactional environments. In this book Mr. Ishizaka provides insight on how to apply Lean operational principles and Kaizen to these dynamic and complicated environments.

ISBN 978-1-926537-08-5 | 2009 | $28.99 | Item: 918

Kaizen and the Art of Creative Thinking

Read the book that New York Times Best Selling author of *The Toyota Way*, Jeffrey Liker says, "will help you understand the deep thinking that underlies the real practice of TPS." Dr. Shigeo Shingo's Scientific Thinking Mechanism is the framework from which Toyota and hundreds of other companies have utilized to manage creative problem solving.

ISBN 978-1-897363-59-1 | 2007 | $59.40 | Item: 909

The Strategos guide to Value Stream & Process Mapping

The Strategos Guide to Value Stream and Process Mapping has proven strategies and helpful tips on facilitating group VSM exercises and puts VSM in the greater Lean context. With photos and examples of related Lean practices, the book focuses on implementing VSM, not just drawing diagrams and graphs.

ISBN 978-1-897363-43-0 | 2007 | $47.00 | Item: 905

The Idea Generator, Quick and Easy Kaizen

The book discusses the Kaizen mind set that enables a company to utilize its resources of the fullest by directly involving all of its manpower in the enhancement and improvement of the productivity of its operations. Published and co-written by Norman Bodek, the Godfather of Lean.

ISBN 978-0971243699 | 2001 | $47.52 | Item: 902

JIT is Flow

Hirano's *5 Pillars o the Visual Workplace* and *JIT Implementation Manual* were classics. They contained detailed descriptions of techniques and clear instructions. This book highlights the depth of the thought process behind Hirano's work. The clarity which Hirano brings to JIT/Lean and the delineation of the principles involved will be invaluable to every leader and manager aiming for business excellence.

ISBN 978-0971243613 | 2007 | $47.52 | Item: 903

Training Materials:
JIT Factory Flow Kit

If your company is serious about implementing a Lean Transformation, every person should go through this training. This hands-on simulation demonstrates the effectiveness of Just in Time manufacturing; it shows how much easier job functions can be and how efficient all employees can become if the simple and easy rules of JIT are followed. It is dynamic enough for high-level management training, yet has enough detail for production staff as well; provides the "Ah-ha, I get it!" factor of all your employees. In less than two hours you will have all your staff agreeing to move to a Lean Production System.

ISBN 978-1-897363-60-7 | 2007 | $479.99 | Item: 1081

5S Training Package

Our 5S Solution Packages will help your company create a sustainable 5S program that will turn your shop floor around and put you ahead of the competition. All of the benefits that come from Lean Manufacturing are built upon a strong foundation of 5S. Enna's solution packages will show you how to implement and sustain an environment of continuous improvement.

Version 1: Sort, Straighten, Sweep, Standardize and Sustain

ISBN 978-0-973750-90-4 | 2005 | $429.99 | Item: 12

Version 2: Sort, Set In Order, Shine, Standardize and Sustain

ISBN 978-1-897363-25-6 | 2006 | $429.99 | Item: 17

To Order:

Mail orders and checks to:
Enna Products Corporation
ATTN: Order Processing
1602 Carolina Street, Unit B3
Bellingham, WA 98229
USA
Phone: (866) 249-7348
Fax: (905) 481-0756
Email: info@enna.com

We accept checks and all major credit cards.

Notice:

All prices are in US Dollars and are subject to change without notice.